AGAINST
ALL ODDS

AGAINST
ALL ODDS

The story of the
Christian Channel Europe

WENDY ALEC

Summit Publishing Ltd

Milton Keynes
England

AGAINST ALL ODDS

British Library Cataloguing-in-Publication data. Catalogue record for this book is available from the British Library.

ISBN: 1-901074-11-0

Scripture taken from the Holy Bible, New King James Version. Copyright © 1979, 1980, 1982 by Thomas Nelson Inc., Publishers. Used by permission.

Cover photograph by Pictor International Ltd.

Ch. 13: Extract from an article by Peter Popham, used by permission from *The Independent on Sunday.*

Reproduced, printed and bound in Great Britain for Summit Publishing Ltd. by Cox & Wyman Ltd., Reading.

96 97 98 99 / 10 9 8 7 6 5 4 3 2 1

Dedication

This book is dedicated to my precious earthly father, Hal 'Doc' Koefman, who has been one of the greatest gifts in my life.

And it is dedicated to my beloved heavenly Father God —the Father after whom all fatherhood is named.

To Him be the glory for great things He has done.

Acknowledgements

Very special thanks to Pauline for her endless patience at finding my documents in strange places in the laptop computer files (when I was convinced all was lost) and for her tireless assistance.

To Beth—who I know went to enormous lengths to set the manuscript. To Noel Halsey who was always a great source of comfort when deadlines were looming and has been a friend to both Rory and me from that first strange but divinely ordained meeting in a restaurant on the M25 (a good place for divine appointments) . . . and lastly but definitely not least—(if I can find her through the reams of paper swathed over her desk and mine) to Linda Finley-Day whom I love dearly, even if she does write me faxes dated "The longest day!" For the strange sense of humour that thankfully we both share that has kept us going through myriads of paperwork; missed deadlines; mislaid endorsements; phonecalls and faxes—and many, many *unforgettable* moments; to many more projects together, Linda!

To so many friends and associates, some mentioned in this book, others who are a part of the story, often in ways they cannot fully know.

And finally, to my wonderful husband—the gift of God in my life, as we continue through this incredible adventure to pioneer this work in Europe together.

May His Kingdom come here in Europe and the world!

Contents

Foreword

*N*o one doubts the power of television. Governments often want to control it for propaganda purposes, advertisers want it to sell their products and journalists want to broadcast their observations and opinions. Indeed all those who try to shape and influence the opinions of others want the access to the masses that television offers. Television is not merely the prime global medium of entertainment it is the greatest communication tool mankind has ever developed.

It is not surprising then that Christians are interested in television. We too have a message and a story to tell. Rather, the mystery is why a book about the rise of Christian television in Europe should be entitled, *Against All Odds*. Surely Christian involvement in television would be taken for granted as European democracy must surely champion the right for the Christian voice to be heard along with every other voice in society. But the facts are otherwise. For instance, until recently Christian television was outlawed in Britain.

In our 'age of tolerance', how come the powers-that-be allow pornography, blasphemy, violence and godless philosophy to flourish but are active against the Christian message? At the press conference of the launch of The Christian Channel Europe, the right of such a channel even to exist was challenged by journalists. It seems that journalists and editors have a right to question and voice their opinion, producers have a right to propagate their beliefs but Christians have not the same right. Actually we have every right to be on television and what's more to break free from the rigidity of traditional religious broadcasting presenting something fresh and new on the European scene.

But the launch of the Channel had more odds stacked against it than merely a cynical press and a television world with its often blatantly anti-Christian stances. Resistance, and at times, outright opposition also came from parts of the Christian religious establishment. In an environment where many European Christian groups are falling over themselves to dissociate from American-style TV evangelism it was felt CCE was too aggressive. Unlike much television CCE is totally up front about the values it propagates and the objects it seeks to achieve. It unashamedly exists to proclaim the Christian gospel. And it is working. Many lives are already being touched and this is only the beginning. The concerns about imbalance are unfounded. For too long the balance has been tipped the other way and CCE is providing a much needed corrective.

CCE's doctrinal stance is thoroughly evangelical and charismatic, without compromise. This emphasis is an accurate reflection of world-wide growing Christianity. And it is not surprising that both liberal and conservative Christian groups are offended. Their approach has failed to stop the Church decline in Europe. It is time for a full-blooded gospel to go forth supported by real Bible-believing teaching to nurture new believers across Europe starved of it. Nominal, watered-down and woolly CCE is definitely not!

That is the background to the story you are about to read. It tells of unlikely beginnings. A young couple plan a major European television initiative from their kitchen table. The humble start of CCE, without finance, without recognition or institutional backing carries the hallmark of the Holy Spirit who inspired, encouraged and carried Rory and Wendy Alec through to one of the greatest Christian successes of Europe in the nineties.

—Pastor Colin Dye, Senior Minister, Kensington Temple

Introduction

This book is dedicated to every Joseph—to every man and woman who has been entrusted with a technicolour dream from God.

You may have been called a young upstart; you may have been thrown in the pit by your 'elder brothers' and labelled presumptuous; you may be serving in Potiphar's house, beset by testings, trials and temptations as the Word of the Lord tests you until God's appointed time for you dawns.

You may be serving solitary confinement in the 'prison' of circumstances—with 'No Way Out' emblazoned all around you in neon letters, surrounded by the barriers of seemingly insurmountable circumstances and obstacles—but take heart, dear dreamer, for on God's appointed day, after all the seeming heartache and disappointments, surely your time will come; and when finally the chief butler remembers you, the gift and calling that God has placed on your life will bring you before Pharaoh just as surely as that other young dreamer before you.

Rory and I had sensed we had a calling on our lives in the area of the media since our early twenties. At a young age, we tasted brief success, and then through the next ten years as the Word of the Lord tested us, we were flung onto the Potter's wheel as a loving heavenly Father started to mould and refine His two young dreamers.

In the early years, we were the epitome of Joseph sporting his marvellous technicolour coat—brimming with vision and assurance, the Father Himself having given us a multicoloured coat of creative talent.

There we were, announcing (like Joseph) in megaphone tones: '*We* have a dream—*we* will affect the nations—*we* will affect the music industry, television and film—millions shall be saved.'

And the heavenly Father, in His infinite wisdom, looked at His technicoloured clothed visionaries, sighed quietly and said: 'It is now time to forge the character integral to the calling that inevitably lies ahead.'

And so the vibrant, technicoloured robe of a spoilt youngest son grew faded under the harshness of the midday sun, and during the years of toil in the wilderness, the brashness and self-confidence of 'I can do for God' was gently tempered into 'God will do for His kingdom.'

Oh yes, we were thrown into the pit of dashed dreams and broken promises early in our dreamer's walk; we were put to serve under Potiphar in the advertising and television production industry; we were forced to flee from the lust of the eyes, lust of the flesh and the deceitfulness of riches. And when we arrived on the shores of Great Britain, we entered our prison years where it seemed that we were doomed to wander in the wilderness, forgotten, with no sense of direction and set to hard labour with little respite. But our God of fathers after whom every father is named, our God of compassion and mercies, looked down upon His young Joseph—Rory and Wendy Alec— and said 'It is time for THE DREAM!'

And as His young, weary servants moved at His command, He gently washed the dust of the wilderness away from our cheeks and wiped the tears from our eyes. And divinely appointed doors began to open as the Lord God Himself started to pave the way for His young dreamers to launch a Christian television channel that would span twenty-four European nations and change the face of religious broadcasting in Europe.

Whether you are in the pit, serving in Potiphar's house or languishing in prison—God has a message for you today: 'Don't give up: your time will come.' For what He has done for Rory and Wendy—through all the seemingly insurmountable obstacles, through all the heartache and disappointment, the laughter and the tears, the mountains and the Red Sea—He will indeed accomplish the same for you.

I pray that as you read these pages the anointing of the Holy Spirit will wash away the dust of discouragement and despair from your mind and heart; that He will revitalise you to fresh hope for the dream that He has placed in *your* heart; that there will be an impartation of the gift of faith, which will strengthen you to face the seemingly impossible circumstances around you, and a supernatural boldness to overcome every demonic assignment and strategy that the enemy has planned to thwart God's dream.

May your heart be comforted, may your soul be encouraged and may the weary arms be strengthened as you walk hand in hand with your Father God until that day when finally *your* time is come and His voice is heard from the heavens: 'Call the dreamer—it is *time* for the dream.'

Wendy Alec

Prophecies

❖   ❖   ❖

*Prophetic word delivered by Jonathan David to Rory
and Wendy Alec in July 1994 at the
Cornerstone Christian Centre*

'*I* *believe very strongly that for both of you, supernatural things
are already happening in the heavens.*

*God shows me that you are like a stone cut out from a
different place and God says I have shaped you, I have formed
you for a divine purpose but like a stone cut out from a different
place, you have tried to fit yourself in so many places that you
have found that you are the unfit stone.*

*But God brought you here that you might become part of
what He is doing here and right across Europe, right across
Germany, right across Russia.*

*And I believe you have, as a couple, a tremendous influence
(on the things) that will take place.*

*People are going to hear about you, even before you ever get
on TV.*

*I don't know if you've been on TV but before you ever do
anything, people are going to have their hearts prepared.*

*I see people even going into the Middle East. This work is
going to go even to the Middle East and there is going to be a
great reservoir of riches.*

*But you are going to establish it on a prophetic vein. It's not
evangelistic only, it's more than just evangelistic. You're going
to establish 'Thus saith the Lord'.*

*This network is going to be producing greater miracles by
turning entire churches. Entire churches are going to be
positioned because of your network.*

Your network is not reaching the unreached alone, but its

going to turn the destiny of the Church. It is going to turn the destiny of the Church.

Where you can't go, where ministers can't go, you'll go and the whole church will turn and when the church turns you will be a shareholder in everything that breaks forth. You will have spiritual dividends.

Jonathan David had never seen Rory and Wendy before and had no prior knowledge of the television project they were involved in at the time.

Prophetic word from Jean Darnell about the rise of Media in Europe

Then I said, 'Lord, what about these streams that go on across the Channel into Europe?'

And He said, 'That represents people who will rise up in the midst of this people movement, this army of witnesses in Britain, whom I will make My communicators.'

Now I hadn't used that word very much before in ministry. I said, 'Lord, what do you mean by communicators?'

And He said, 'They will not only be people endowed with the gifts of the Holy Spirit, with strong faith, but they will also be people talented in the arts. They will be writers, musicians, singers and actors, and also technicians in television, radio and the mass media. I will call and send them and put them in strategic places. I will bless their natural talents with My Spirit, and they will be good: *they will excel. They will be leaders in their fields. I will send them into Europe, where they will meet other people in the media, and through them I will release the word of God very fast in Europe. The result will be another wave of a spiritual awakening, with thousands coming to Christ throughout Europe.'*

From Revival *by Hugh Black, published by New Dawn, 1993.*

Chapter One

❖ ❖ ❖

Roots

I was born in late January in Welbeck Street in London,
England. As I'm slightly older than Rory I'll indulge in some
creative licence and omit the year. Let's just say I fit in the thirty-
something bracket!

My father, fondly called 'Doc' by all near and dear, was a
physician with a flourishing practice in the heart of London's
medical profession—Wimpole Street. At forty-five he started
his second family with me, his long-awaited little girl, and he
was a gift from God even at that early stage of my life.

My mother, Jean, nineteen years younger than my father,
was a tough, fiery, practical lady. A born administrator
and organiser, she grew up in the hard North of England,
in Leeds. She was a fighter with a unique brand of self-
sufficiency, having had to fend for herself at a young age.
There was little of the philosopher about the pragmatic young

Jean, but then again, my father more than made up for that.

The charming Dr Koefman possessed all the unique qualities that were inherently present in his Jewish heritage. His brilliant academic mind and genteel English manner belied his underlying creative nature which revealed itself in his life-long love of classical music and art. 'All in a day's work' for Daddy meant running his medical practice before studying Russian, playing the violin and reading *Decline and Fall of the Roman Empire* to unwind.

But the attribute that most affected my young life, (apart from his most incredible sense of humour) was the unfailing compassion he displayed to all his patients, regardless of status. There were many nights when he would stay up with a patient who had cancer or who was terminally ill and the next day just look at my mother (who of course looked after the administration of the practice) and gently shake his head, which translated meant, 'Don't charge them, Jean.'

His only earthbound weakness was a passion for his Jaguar cars, which he did indulge in for most of my childhood years, but Daddy had long learned that to give meant to receive.

So there I was—a typical British doctor's daughter and no doubt fairly spoiled!

'Daddy's girl', I was educated in a private school in Surrey where I learned the violin, took ballet and singing and was taken to West End first nights of opera, ballet and theatre, all from the age of four. My younger brother had entered this scenario when I was two and from all accounts, I was not particularly amused. God bless you, Robert!

Then at the age of eight, destiny entered and my parents made a decision to emigrate to South Africa. God in his Divine over-view ensured that this little English girl landed in Durban, South Africa—a whole continent away—and so a new life began.

I was enrolled in an all-girls Catholic convent presided over by German nuns, as my parents felt that this offered the best academic standard.

My parents were extremely strict (especially my mother) and were insistent on high grades and good behaviour. Up until the age of thirteen, I was the most disciplined, conscientious, hard-working and well-behaved student in class. But the term that high school began, the decay set in or, as my parents said, 'Teenagitis' began.

My schoolwork deteriorated as I started to gravitate more and more towards Speech and Drama and Music. This did not bode well for a child who was being groomed by her parents to be a doctor. As High School progressed, I became the class clown and rebel. I was cheeky, incredibly strong-minded and started to buck authority. I was late for classes. My middle name was 'trouble'.

In my final year, I behaved so badly that I was demoted as a prefect and sat languishing in detention, much to my conservative parents' horror. This was not how a 'doctor's daughter' should behave!

But during all my rebellious teenage years, I was hungry for God. At the age of eleven, I had been to a school mass at the Catholic convent where the priest had held up a picture of Jesus and the Sacred Heart. In my heart, always longing after God, I had said: 'God, if you give each of us a picture, I will *know* that you love me and I will be yours for ever.' Although there were several hundred of us there, each one of us were given a picture of Jesus . . . and I never forgot this act of God.

The next year, Billy Graham came out to Durban. I went up in the altar call. My heart longed for God and with a childlike faith I committed my life to Jesus . . . but I had *no* teaching. I didn't understand salvation.

After matriculating from the convent, I was enrolled at Natal University in Durban. My behaviour went from bad to worse. I was sleeping late, skipping lectures, tanning on the beach or on the balcony all day and then partying at night. And this was *every* night, till four or five in the morning.

There was something in my nature that needed to thrive on risk. Risk in relationship, in habits, in lifestyle . . . and it started to take its toll.   My parents received a letter from the Dean of the University which actually stated, 'We *despair* of Wendy's behaviour'.

Needless to say, due to too much partying and no work, I failed my second year of university. My normally calm and self-controlled British father reverted to his far more passionate Middle Eastern roots and excommunicated me from the family! To him, I was as dead. I did not exist.

I was a month short of my eighteenth birthday.

Things went downhill and I degenerated into the night clubs and the music scene. I was mixing primarily with male musicians, and I was involved in several relationships at once, some of the men being married. They would buy me my cigarettes, take me to dinner and encourage my song-writing career. I was acting just like a bimbo and lapping it up avidly. I didn't care who was hurt. All I cared about was gratification for the moment and I was loving it.

(*Take hope for all your wayward teenagers, parents.*) I was so wild that the local charismatic church found me two nice, unsuspecting Christian families to try and bring me into some order. Neither of them succeeded in 'taming' me as I drove both families up the wall by continually breaking out at night!

A music producer formed a music group for me and we started serious rehearsals on my repertoire of songs. I was now enrolled at drama college and staying in a girl's youth hostel.

The end of the year found me finishing off a set in a night club and singing the oldie 'Cocaine' by J. J. Kale when one of the 'conservative', strait-laced Christians came to seek me out.

Being by nature dramatic and creative, I had always felt that I could never fit into this strict and virtuous Christian mould.

'Ms Strait-lace' (looking like a Pear's soap advert)

cornered me in the ladies' room where I glared at her grimly from over my cigarette holder (looking like a more dubious kind of ad!) and with tears brimming over, she confronted me: 'What are you doing to Jesus?'

An intense anger rose within me. I wanted to lash out at her. She finally left and I was alone facing my reflection.

Suddenly, the room was filled, saturated with the presence of Almighty God. Very slowly, I looked up into the mirror and I saw the Lord Jesus Christ. I remember instinctively wanting to run away, thinking He was going to be so angry with me because my life was in such a mess.

But you know, Jesus looked at me and oh, how He loved me. Through all the years that have passed, I have never forgotten that moment.

It was His eyes. They were filled with such tender mercy and compassion. His eyes literally blazed with a passion and a love for me . . . And all the while, tears were running down His face.

Instead of judgement and condemnation, the Lord Jesus was crying for me.

In that split second, I discovered a love that would fill the vacuum inside me that I'd been trying so desperately to fill with relationships, highs and challenges.

I finally surrendered my life to the Lord Jesus Christ . . . and it was completely turned around in an instant. Wild as I had been, my life was transformed and revival started to sweep through my dormitory of rebel friends at the hostel.

The only people who were unconvinced by my dramatic conversion were the tight-knit group of Christians—the 'Pharisees and Sadducees' on the next floor—who proceeded to stare at me on occasion in the lift with that severe 'whitewashed sepulchured' glare, because they knew that I was holding Bible studies while I was still smoking!

How grateful I am that God doesn't judge people on the

outside. In the Amplified translation, it says that Jesus ate with the *pre-eminently* wicked and oh—how I love that. That is why on some of our publicity (as in our advert in the *Sky* magazine we wrote—GOD'S NOT IN A BOX—HE'S ON THE BOX!)

Oh—how much God loves *all* people. He's not as concerned with the externals as most of us tend to be. He bypasses that and goes straight to the heart.

Now remember, I'm not condoning smoking. I'm saying that God deals with all of us in different ways at different times, and when our hearts are truly surrendered to Him and we grow in the Word of God, the externals will come into line with the change in our spirit and soul. God majors on the inside, not the externals . . . *always.*

And so, an intense desire was birthed in my heart to reach the 'real' world—the secular world—people who found it hard to relate to 'church' and 'religion'. I already sensed deeply—at this very early stage of my Christian walk—that one of the most powerful ways to achieve this was by music and 'drama' (the only media tools I knew or understood at that stage).

A few weeks later, I found myself seated in front of Nellie Roberts, married to Pastor Fred Roberts of the Durban Christian Centre. (I still looked more as if I had been dragged out of the nearest smoke-filled club, dressed in my tight black leather outfit, than having an appointment with a pastor's wife!) How gracious that lady was to me. There I was, stubbing out cigarette after cigarette into her rubbish bin, and there she was, just loving me with the love of Jesus.

Well, Nellie just loved me . . . and then she prophesied. That was fifteen years ago—and these words from the prophecy were branded in my soul.

'And you shall be raised up as a forerunner of creative evangelism in this generation.'

And so, I started on a collision course with God's destiny for my life. And in the years to come, God was to train up both Rory and me and open our eyes to what I believe to be one of the most powerful evangelistic tools on earth in these last days—*the Media.*

Chapter Two

❖ ❖ ❖

Enter Rory

*I*n January 1981, I enrolled in a discipleship training course at Youth With a Mission in Scotland and went on to join a church in Sussex.

In the winter of 1982, I returned to South Africa to enrol at Rhema Bible College. And oh—what precious years followed. The next five years were what I call my 'wonder years', years when I was privileged to be totally set apart and separated to the Lord.

For months I was able to lock myself away and spend hour after hour alone with the Holy Spirit. Many afternoons I would be found face down at the back of Rhema Bible Church, interceding, in between following up the Rhema Sunday service born-again responses and counselling people with needs. I was also involved with a multi-racial singing group travelling around South Africa, praying for the sick and ministering in a very young, prophetic anointing.

Sometimes, I have to confess, in the hectic, pressurised lifestyle of the Christian Channel and the sleepless nights amid nappies and dummies, I look back longingly on those wonder years!

The angels were no doubt working hard, for one weekend— in God's blueprint—I was invited to minister at a church in the small mining town of Rustenburg.

'I don't want to *go* to Rustenburg!' I stated to my long-standing friend, Annie.

She looked at me with the glint of God in her eye.

'You *need* to go.'

I arrived at the morning service and there, leading the praise and worship, was a vibrant young man who played the keyboards in a manner that immediately got my attention.

This talented young man's name was Rory Alec.

Rory was born Rory Alec Stephen in the small mining town of Rustenburg, South Africa.

His mother, Lona, at 22 was an unusual, independent young woman, who had been estranged from Rory's natural father even before his birth.

Robert Stephen, Rory's father, a James Dean lookalike, although bright and extremely charming, was at that stage a rather selfish man who had been pampered and was used to his own way. After the marriage breakdown, when Rory was just a few months old, Lona moved away from the Transvaal, back down to Durban to continue her career as a radiographer. Rory, blissfully unaware of the emotional break-up, was looked after in the hospital nursery. The family's memories are of a contented, adaptable, sunny infant adored by young and old alike.

When Rory was one, he gained a new stepfather, Paul Jordaan—a genuine, kind man. Almost straight away, a brother and a sister were born. Deep down Rory started to feel that he was the outsider. Unfortunately after only a short time of marriage there was an amicable separation. Rory was just five years old.

Lona and the children moved back up to Rustenburg where her father owned a farm, the scene of many memorable childhood weekends. But it was at the local hospital that Lona's destiny was about to change for ever.

Stanley Perrins, a newly qualified physiotherapist, had just arrived to take up a post at the local hospital in Rustenburg. Suffering from a degenerative eye disease, he was already 80 per cent blind. Stan was one of those rare finds in today's society— solid gold. His keen mind was coupled with a code of unparalleled integrity and honour. Stan was unflappable, perceptive and literally the salt of the earth! Although Lona was not by any means interested in *any* relationship, they became friends and in 1972, when Rory was eight, they were married. Rory, having had no contact with his natural father, was adopted by Stan and everyone finally settled down into a stable family life.

School was basically a non-event for Rory. He was not by any means an academic and preferred to spend his leisure time involved in music, which had been his passion since boyhood. His mother, sensing her son's natural musical aptitude, invested in an organ and Rory began music lessons. By the age of fourteen he was playing the piano and keyboards, drums, guitars—literally anything that made a sound! It was an unusual musical gift, and in time it would start to open doors in the South African music and advertising industry. But for the meantime, school was to be endured.

Then teenagehood struck with a vengeance.

Rory was far more conservative than me and never had my tendency to kick over the traces. He found himself facing a different form of temptation.

A clash of wills arose in the household between stepfather Stan and the young Rory. The sound of harsh words,

slamming doors and flaring tempers raged day after day for
months on end.

During this volatile and emotionally unstable period of home
life, Rory found himself profoundly impressed by a new
exchange student at school, Warren Edminster. Warren always
seemed calm and unruffled by circumstances around him.
However, he approached Rory for advice about his girlfriend
problems and Rory, in turn, started to ask some leading
questions about this 'born-again thing'. They got together for a
lunch of burgers and milkshakes. Rory dealt with the girlfriend
problems in five minutes then listened to Warren witness to him
for the rest of the afternoon.

Rory ended up one evening in a prayer meeting led by André
and Cliff Scott. At the end of the evening, André sensed strongly
that a young person wanted to give their heart to the Lord Jesus
and asked if they would please raise their hand. Rory, to his
initial dismay, found that his hand had gone up.

That evening in a small housegroup, surrounded by the love
of Jesus, Rory prayed the sinner's prayer from his heart, and
committed his life to Jesus.

The next day at school, after hearing what had happened to
him, Rory's friends started to mock him, saying, 'So, now you're
an angel', but by the end of the day, they had become intrigued
by the unmistakable change in his language and behaviour.
Victor, one of Rory's friends, proceeded to give his life to Jesus
and needless to say, many others in Rory's school were born
again.

And two years after his conversion, I arrived at the church in
Rustenburg . . . and there was Rory leading praise and worship!

Now, Rory was still serving in the South African Defence
Force and had this remarkably short haircut. And I had always
simply loved guys with *long* hair. So Rory immediately had a
strike against him, courtesy of the Armed Forces.

But Rory started to call me and he didn't stop calling. The

fact that he was also a brilliant musician made it extremely difficult for me to ignore him. (Actually he was very cute!)

Then the pastor's wife dropped a bombshell.

'Oh,' she said casually, 'Rory believes that God has said that you're to be his wife!'

In fact Rory had gone to his pastor the day before I arrived and said that God had said that he would meet his wife the next day. I have to admit that I *did* get a fright at this unexpected comment, as Rory was younger than me.

But, by this time, we had got a Christian musical group together and were faithfully driving the neighbours and Rory's parents near to dementia by practising the entire rock opera repertoire every weekend.

And so, praise the Lord, Rory eventually finished his army service and grew his hair (*very* long, actually)—much to my conservative mother's horror.

God had brought together two young Christians, who loved each other and the Lord Jesus with all their hearts, with a vision to reach out to the world through creative evangelism. Actually, I must qualify that . . . an *enormous* vision.

You see, the one thing that Rory and I never queried, even at such a young stage of our relationship, was the fact that God had called us to affect nations and that the calling on our lives would change the world. There was never a flicker of doubt in our minds. Even at that infantile stage, God had said the vision would go from Johannesburg to London and eventually to Los Angeles.

And as we grew in the Word through the years, it became evident that this absolute assurance and conviction that God could use us as 'little David' to impact the media (Goliath) was actually the gift of faith in operation.

And we both had a strong but unchanging sensing in our spirits that this destiny for us was to start in the United Kingdom.

A few months later, Rory was discharged from the army after successfully completing two years of military service. Earlier that year, he had received seven thousand rand from an inheritance. Without hesitation, he invested it in the recording of the title track from the rock opera, *We Want Our Money Back*. It was time to go public.

In grand style, we embarked on what would be the norm in our later careers and calling—a Presentation Evening, to share the vision with hopefully wide-eyed onlookers who would catch it.

A friend of ours in catering, enthused by the vision of the rock opera, donated the use of his restaurant for the evening, which we packed out with every friend, relative, relatives' friend and any other rather unsuspecting guest who had most probably been lured there by the promise of a decent meal, rather than because of our supposedly budding talent!

Let me mention here, that by this time, Rory had been reunited with his natural father and a profound reconciliation had taken place. So that evening, Bob Stephen was one of our special guests.

Well, the lights were dimmed and the sound went on (extremely loudly)—we had the audio in those days but lacked the visual. The parents looked very proud, the friends looked proud, (if they didn't they wouldn't get dinner) and the secular record company representative stared round in a state of unease, if not alarm. (He *had* been warned it was a Christian event.) However, the evening ran its course and the previously extremely hungry and very bored 'Christian lady' (who was known to raise inordinately large sums of money for secular film projects) suddenly had a mood swing. Her eyes started to sparkle with what we desperately hoped was the recognition of 'raw' talent . . .

So much did her eyes shine, that within a few months, several million rand had been raised for three gospel musical projects, one of which was ours.

To cut a long story short, we became engaged and were married on January 10, 1987 in Durban. We honeymooned in the Eastern Transvaal.

We were paid twenty thousand rand just to appear in our own music video. Immediately after our honeymoon, we were flown to the south of France to MIDEM, Europe's most prestigious music festival.

There followed five-star hotels in Nice and Cannes . . . posters . . . presentation packs . . . next stop, London. Pocket money, dinners, and a quick indoctrination into London's West End to prepare us for our project to come. We saw *Time, Cats, Les Miserables, Me and My Girl, Starlight Express, Chess* and *Phantom of the Opera.* Rory had just turned twenty-one—the rising Christian media evangelists were on course and about to learn some *valuable* lessons.

On our arrival back in Johannesburg, we went straight into the music studio to start working on the full rock opera album. Rory and I wrote the music, I wrote the lyrics and Rory and Nikki Saks arranged the musical tracks.

During the next three months, however, the music projects changed in the producers' minds from Ministry to Business . . . and oh, what a subtle but dangerous shift this was. Strife between the producers set in and within a few weeks the project disintegrated, with many question marks as to the legal appropriation of funds.

And so, Rory and I, Tom Ingles and Pierre De Chamois were left as the unsuspecting Christian artists in a shambles of broken promises and commitments, lawyers and accountants. Greed and selfish ambition had destroyed the birthing of what we believed to be potentially one of the most progressive and far-reaching Christian media projects of the eighties.

But in the maze of shattered dreams, Father God comforted us, saying—'This is where you're *going*. . . now I'm going to help you to grow up and train you up.' And God started to put us through His own training process to build the character and steadfastness that surely was integral to all that would lie in wait for us.

Desperate to continue to generate a living, we burst our way into the life of one of South Africa's best-loved secular comedians—Eddie Eckstein (the South African equivalent of Lenny Henry). Eddie had a bunch of midi-gear (musical recording equipment) standing in amongst his comedy library and research material in the cellar under the house.

'We'll make it work for you, Eddie!' we enthused. And with Eddie an aghast onlooker, we proceeded to turn the bits and pieces into a workable studio.

Our career in the secular media gingerly lurched forward. And although we didn't understand why God would seemingly place us in the secular media world, when we so desperately wanted to be involved in Christian projects, God in His magnificent overview was starting to train us up for the future.

We started out by selling our wares to the cut-throat advertising industry. Within a couple of months, we were regularly writing music and lyrics for the ad agencies. Commissioned to write radio jingles for them, we produced material for corporate launches and cabaret shows.

One morning during this period, 22-year-old Rory had a bright idea in the bath. South Africa had suffered severe floods. With visions of Bob Geldof floating on the horizon, he uttered—'Let's create a flood album.'

And they did. Eddie and Rory became executive producers on one of South Africa's most remarkable projects. Two long-playing record albums were launched in aid of the 1988 South African disaster fund. Rory and Eddie organised a major campaign to promote the sale of the flood albums and co-ordinated sixty-four companies from all over Johannesburg and South Africa to sponsor the entire campaign.

Soon after that, one of our most loyal clients approached us, offering us a wonderful remuneration package if we would only come and work for their agency.

Our advertising career began.

Rory became agency radio and TV producer, and I became copywriter. God took us from concentrating on just the musical gifting that He had placed in us and started to expand our creative talents in the secular world.

God looked on us with great favour and we were soon promoted to middle management, working on national campaigns across South Africa for clients such as French Connection/ Jordache, National Panasonic and Pizzahut, learning the vital aspects of combining the USPs (Unique Selling Points) with highly creative concepts to gain universal appeal.

Then came the introduction of television in the form of the production of agency television commercials. God in His preparation started to marry the audio and the visual together, preparing us for the mammoth tasks ahead.

But God's vision for the media still burned in our hearts. We sensed that God had called us to an apostolic, prophetic media ministry—encompassing television, film and music—that would not only affect the Christian world, but would have a major impact on everyone else.

It was during this time in advertising after the heartache of the Christian music project that we cried out to God, 'Father, confirm our calling. Give us a sign that you have indeed called us to affect the face of the media in this generation.'

Almost immediately, we received a phone call from South Africa's equivalent of the BBC, the SABC (South African Broadcasting Corporation) saying that the music video from the rock opera produced from the Christian music project had been nominated in the secular Telefunken Top Music Video of the Year Awards. (We hadn't even known that it had been entered.)

This was like being nominated for a Christian song on *Top of the Pops*. A one in a million!

We arrived at the SABC studios on the day of the awards with no record company, no agent or manager amidst all the heavyweight secular groups and their heavyweight entourages.

And when the winner was announced, it was . . . Rory Alec for 'Mr X'.

The press had a field day with the headline: 'Unknown wins top music award'. We won fifteen thousand rand.

Once again, God had confirmed our calling in the midst of the 'unbelievers'. What constantly seemed to distinguish us from those around us involved in 'church media' was the fact that the acclaim or recognition for the giftings in our lives was coming from the 'world' rather than from the church.

A year later, the agency broke their profit share arrangement with us and we were led, we believe now, by the Holy Spirit, into the wilderness of the television commercial production industry, to be tempted by the devil.

Chapter Three

❖   ❖   ❖

The Power and the Glory

*I*t was now the end of 1988. We were still faithfully attending Rhema Bible Church in Johannesburg with the vision for the media and Britain burning like a flame in our hearts.

At every invitation for those called to full-time ministry, Rory and I would zealously rush up to the front of the church. But for all our commitment to God to be used in Christian media and move to the United Kingdom, the doors continued to open for us in the secular media industry in South Africa. We would have to be patient and wait for God's perfect timing.

Now it was time for us to enter the cut-throat, dog-eat-dog world of cinema and television commercial production where only the fittest or the most capitalised survive.

When we launched Alec-Gene Productions (our television commercial production house), there were about a hundred production houses servicing the sophisticated advertising industry in Johannesburg. Approximately ten to twelve of these could be termed major players.

We started at position number one hundred and one and by the time we hit our glorious demise, we had successfully hyped, busked and marketed ourselves into the Top Ten.

To succeed in the highly competitive industry of television commercial production, we needed either a film director who could rank with the best, as we had to 'pitch' for commercial work, or we needed an inordinate amount of chutzpah!

Needless to say, we had the latter.

The entrepreneur in each of us raced ahead in our zest to conquer the South African advertising industry and Sandton, the mecca of Johannesburg's major advertising agencies, was the place to be. In our finite minds, we decided that *obviously* God was going to raise Alec-Gene Productions as a beacon of light in the industry. We would then open a London branch and so—*we* (Joseph with the megaphone) would finance Christian media projects.

All nice and cosy and comfortable: this plan completely eradicated the looming possibility that we might have to go to London by faith. Lord, preserve us! Ours was a much better plan. We would make a couple of hundred thousand rand, preferably more, and then relocate to London (to take over the film industry, naturally!).

And so . . . with this logic in mind, and believing that God was with Alec-Gene Productions, we flexed our empire-building muscles and burst forth onto the unsuspecting tight-knit, cynical, arrogant production industry.

To fill you in, cinema and television commercial production in Johannesburg was basically the 'yuppie' side of television. In comparison with production for the state-owned television (SABC) and the relatively infantile film industry in South Africa, serious television commercial production involved putting a huge amount of money, time and co-ordination into thirty seconds' worth of product.

Many of South Africa's commercials were recognised at both the highly prestigious British and American commercial awards. It was an industry filled with ambitious, upwardly mobile, highly talented and grossly overpaid film directors and producers. (Many were on cocaine, with expense accounts in the stylish Sandton restaurants that matched the expense-leased sports cars they drove.) And they all had one overriding ambition—to *make it*.

In late 1988, we joined the ranks of the Perrier-sipping, Gucci-clad, Sandton commercial crowd to make our mark. Commercials had to be 'won' from the advertising agency. We immediately descended on the fifty-two advertising agencies to 'pitch' for work, with what we considered to be an inspirational marketing idea.

Our production secretary was an ex-make up artist. So we had her fill fifty-two glass vials with make-up blood and place them on cotton wool in small glossy black boxes with the label—'FRESH BLOOD IN THE MARKET-PLACE'.

Apart from the reaction of a few paranoid creative directors (who thought the blood was a death threat), where other production companies had laboured for years to become known, *we* achieved instant recognition in the advertising agency arena. All eyes were suddenly glued to this young, upstart production house.

This was combined with the wild report that Rhema and Pastor Ray MacCauley was financing the production house. (Not true!)

Word now spread like wildfire in Johannesburg's advertising industry that 'the *Christians*' were among the heathen.

Now we were confronted with our first challenge—the advertising agencies admired our innovation and flair, but would our film production be good enough for them to entrust us with our first commercial?

Enter Nik a young creative music video director and a talented but volatile free spirit. He would work for us but refused to sign anything contractually. Having already painstakingly gone through what felt like hundreds of uninspiring young director's showreels, we reluctantly agreed to these terms, believing that there was enough raw talent in Nik to get the agencies' attention.

Rory and I took a deep breath and cut together a showreel that we desperately hoped would 'peel the faces' off the 'jaded, seen-it-all-before' advertising agencies. Much to our relief, it did and so we won our first commercial.

One commercial led to the next and very soon we were being viewed as the 'up and coming', 'the bratpack', the 'newcomers to watch'. Before our eventual demise, some even labelled us potentially *the* production house of the nineties. Budgets ran from one hundred thousand to three hundred thousand rand per commercial.

As executive producers, Rory and I were responsible for all aspects of production from all budgeting and financial aspects of television production through to the co-ordination of all producers, film directors, production managers, crew, cast, props, locations, studios, camera and lighting equipment hire, vehicle hire, film processing, editing, music and post-production.

The business leased a large house in the exclusive Johannesburg suburb of Sandton, with a swimming pool and tennis court, set in large grounds where our two ridgebacks roamed. (We were upwardly mobile, remember . . . the upwardly mobile in South Africa owned ridgebacks!) They were simply gorgeous dogs who were treated like our babies. (Nik was also vehemently anti-yuppie but had a strange affection for us, which surpassed even his brand of intellectualising.)

Well, the saga progresses. Our personal house was an unusual six-bedroom, three-bathroom thatched house in Bryanston and to complete the total picture, we were driving a brand new BMW cabriolet and a gleaming old black Daimler.

Over the months, we started to build up credibility including the production of several high-budget, high-profile commercials for a model agency, a well-known brand of designer sunglasses and the launch of a British newspaper into South Africa. We even landed the new 'South African Police' commercial for a new South Africa.

Meanwhile, all types were parading through the production offices, some of them rather strange characters. This included one extremely talented young film lighting cameraman (the flavour of the month in the industry) who used to arrive in his huge old black Mercedes, reminiscent of a hearse. Completely strung out on cocaine, he would pour out his addictive woes and, on occasion, challenge us to get him converted.

Towards the end of 1990, wild rumours started to circulate that the lady heading up one of the crew agencies was a witch and had put a curse on us because we were Christians.

And almost to convince us, disaster struck.

The South African political situation with the tribal wars had created a highly volatile business climate and suddenly the big businesses started to cut back dramatically on their advertising budgets. The first thing in their advertising briefs to go were . . . guess what? . . . yes: television commercials.

Clients were happy to keep what in the industry is labelled the 'below the line', but the costly above the line sphere of high-budget television commercials was the first to disappear.

And the production houses that would suffer most were the new, young, brave houses that had minimal capital resources to ride the storm.

Now, we had also just finished shooting a music video for Mango Groove (one of South Africa's top music groups) with Nik. And then it happened . . . The 'big boys' (the most heavy-weight production house in Johannesburg) offered Nik a deal that he couldn't and *didn't* refuse.

And so he exited . . . with some of our clients in tow.

Suddenly we were left sans the one commodity that we had invested all our time and energy in—*Nik*.

Enter two more middle-of-the-road, experienced film directors . . . and their expense accounts, their long lunches . . . producers . . . production managers . . . the list went on.

There was just one slight problem. Our overheads had doubled, but our film directors were spending more time 'doing lunch' with our clients than actually bringing the work in or tying any adverts down.

We started off in 1991 pitching on 2.2 million rand worth of advertising commercials. Normally we would win at least forty per cent of this. We were awarded the 'Pick and Pay' (the South African equivalent of Sainsbury's) commercial worth over a quarter of a million rand. A week later, because of the political climate, they postponed until the following year.

We were devastated. That commercial would have taken us through the rocky months to March.

Finally, we were awarded one more commercial worth one hundred and fifty thousand rand. But at that stage, we were already trimming overheads frantically and had given some of our key staff notice. This included the film director nominated by the agency to shoot this commercial. To cut a long story short, he and his producer walked off with the advert.

Weary and exhausted from extinguishing minor and major fires, we decided not to go through the legal wrangle and concentrated our energies on pitching for a new airline account, which was also postponed.

By this time, if we were honest, we would admit that our aim had now become a desire to get to the top and to make as much money as possible while getting there, rather than to honour God in the industry. Pride comes before destruction . . . and so the seeds had been sown.

Things went from bad to worse. Our Daimler was stolen. Our bank manager, who had been our most enthusiastic backer, (we had given him Richard Branson's biography to encourage him!) finally started to pull the rug.

Whereas before, anything that we touched had turned to gold, now it seemed that there was only destruction all around us.

No matter where we tried to dam up the holes, or how we tried to rescue the sinking ship, nothing worked. There was a supernatural slamming of the door on any more of our upwardly mobile ventures and no matter how much we sought God or practically addressed the situation, there was no doubt about it—Alec Gene was dead.

Because of our unwillingness to arrive in England with no security and by faith, we had been, in the permissive will of God, building up a house that was our own and not in the plan of God. We had been labouring in vain.

Even so, in the midst of the seeming defeat, favour was still round about us. We could have had a 'bankruptcy' party and our clients would have come! Our creditors gave us grace beyond measure. It was almost as though everyone agreed that undoubtedly destiny was hovering over us, but it was to be in a different sphere.

By this time, I was six months pregnant. We lost our exclusive office furniture worth thousands of rand. We lost our beautiful house, our BMW (the Daimler was already stolen), the computers, fax machines, photocopiers, company vans and cars. Eventually circumstances were so pitiful that I ended up selling my clothes to be able to pay our faithful Josie. Oh—how the mighty had fallen!

We arrived in desperation at Rory's parents' house in Rustenburg with our ridgebacks in tow. Rory was still just twenty-five. We didn't even have money for an airticket to the UK.

We had lost *everything*.

Rory was by this stage so numbed that he would sit in front of the computer for hours at a time. I was seven-and-a-half months pregnant with no knowledge of what next month held, let alone tomorrow.

The dream was shattered.

The twenty-fifth of August came and with it, a gorgeous nine-pound girl, Samantha Jean. She was a face presentation and after an almost full labour, I had to have an emergency caesarean. After the operation, I was desperately ill with an infection.

Rory and I were completely shell-shocked. *What* was *happening* to us?

We sensed that we had great things to achieve for God. We knew we were called—there was a specific destiny on our lives—but chaos was all around us. Where was God's plan? All we had ever wanted to do was to serve Him and work for Him. No matter how involved we had been in secular media, we had always wanted His will—but now what?

There was seemingly no sense, no comfort, no direction. And so, we cried out to the Lord: 'Make a way where there seems to be no way.' And somewhere deep in our hearts in the midst of the horror and the pressure of closed doors, there was this spark that whispered 'and now into the will of God'.

Chapter Four

❖ ❖ ❖

The Wasteland
or
How the Mighty Have Fallen

And so—dear readers—that is how the great and mighty, now the greatly fallen, happened to land in England in the late September of 1991. We stood on my parents' doorstep in Dorset (minus the ridgebacks) looking like ex-inmates of Belsen in our pallor, clutching our three-week-old baby and the princely fortune of eight hundred pounds with a desperate air.

Much to my parents' relief, (my father had offered the garden shed as a alternative place of residence if the baby continued to wake everyone five times a night) we managed to find a tiny two-bedroom flat in Thames Ditton, Surrey. Unfortunately the owners were not prepared to let us use the second bedroom, so we all slept together, which also meant that we all woke together whenever Samantha (our baby) woke—oh hallelujah!

In the midst of this, there was great activity to try and keep Rory in England. (I had a British passport, Rory didn't.) After much fervent intensive prayer in front of the counters at the Home Office, at which I'm sure people thought we were muttering in Afrikaans, Rory was given the official stamp to stay in the United Kingdom indefinitely.

Then there was the next obstacle—how to survive.

While we had been producing commercials, a desire to see the gospel preached through A-grade Hollywood films had grown in our hearts. We felt God had given us three major projects including a project called 'The AntiChrist'.

At this stage, we were not in any way, interested in implementing Christian television. We considered it to be primarily fairly insular by nature and our burning desire was to *reach* the lost.

Unfortunately, a short time after our arrival in the UK it became apparent that the film industry in the UK was not only struggling but fighting for its very survival. Anyhow, I managed to get myself a London film agent, and we linked up with a London design studio for the animated project and started to write a serious screenplay.

During this time, Rory met a fellow Christian brother at the church we had joined and they decided (which I will always believe was God's permissive will) to collaborate on some sports promotions in the now re-opening New South Africa as a means of raising some serious money.

After they had made an initial trip back to South Africa, the sports plans took a turn towards music promotions and they started to research the possibilities of taking music groups out to a South Africa that had been starved of any international inter-action for years.

So, while Rory and his colleague were plotting and planning

their tours to South Africa, I was involved in the first few rewrites of a hundred and twenty pages of screenplay amidst nappies, bottles and decorating the flat lemon and blue (to get some relief from the mottled brown and purple carpet).

Also in this period, we attended two courses on professional Hollywood screenplay writing in London overseen by Ron Suppa, a tutor at UCLA (the University of Los Angeles) and producer of Sylvester Stallone's movie *Paradise Alley*.

We took the liberty of inviting Ron for lunch. He turned to us and said 'I *never* do this . . . but I will.' And so, over the months, a friendship grew and in fact he will be co-producing our first live action animated screenplay.

The next step was Rory, myself and Samantha taking off for South Africa. Rory was taking Shakatak, the jazz fusion music group on a South African tour spanning the five-thousand-seater arenas in Johannesburg, Durban and Cape Town. Rory (the producer) was to set it up and his partner (the accountant) was to monitor it from London until two weeks before. Let me just say here—if you ever wanted a definition of gambling, it is called *music tours!*

In addition, Rory was about to experience an unparalleled crisis of faith. He had been born again at sixteen, but had up till this time lived quite a superficial Christian life. Often it had seemed that there was a barrier to his spiritual growth which had always been beyond my understanding.

Because I had always needed God so desperately, I had been consumed with Him since that night of recommitment many years before, but Rory had always seemed to skim the surface with God. There were many times that I cried out in desperation for God to change Rory into His man but there was little visible transformation.

And so, there was Rory, fighting with God, fighting with himself and being lured into the glitzy world of secular promoting.

Well, I was praying so long and so hard . . . The one thing that I was totally convinced of, was that my heavenly Father was not going to leave *any* stone unturned until this situation was brought to account.

Things became so pressurised that I almost returned to England, but God told me to stay and be strong. The tours started, and the press across South Africa raved about the concerts.

There was only one thing that would or could get Rory's attention in his present state and I knew exactly what that was . . . and so did God . . . it was the *money.*

Rory's business partner came out and was shocked at the way Rory was behaving and at his hardness of heart. His behaviour spiralled progressively downward and then, as the last show was completed in the prestigious Ellis Park, amidst glowing reports and packed arenas, it appeared there had been a strategic mistake in setting up the tour—they were several performances too short.

If there were no extra concerts, they would lose a vast amount of money . . . and it was too *late* to change it.

God finally burst the balloon. The tour lost approximately seventy thousand pounds. God now had the hook He needed to start to pull Rory back in. This was because it was Rory personally who had raised the initial capital from the Christian investors and felt honour-bound not to let them down.

And so, he returned to England, still fighting with God, but with his back against the wall. In fact, I would say that God slammed his nose full face *into* the wall!

You see, no one is exempt from deception, dear friend. Deception is deception because it *is* deceiving, and up to that time, Rory had been a spiritual baby. But then he turned full face around and repented—a genuine, deep repentance and a true surrender. And probably for the very first time, God started to have proper access to his life.

Unfortunately, the pastor of the church we were attending

took the attitude 'Get in the Word'. There was very little pastoring or getting alongside Rory. No personal ministry. He inferred that Rory should sit on the back row for at least six months and that they would watch his 'fruit'. In layman's terms, he was putting Rory '*on ice*'.

Oh, but the ways of God are not the ways of man. How far superior are the purposes and plans of our heavenly Father. Where a man will look at the exterior, we have a God who sees through to the intents and purposes of the heart. How grateful Rory and I are for that.

Almost immediately, the pastors of Cornerstone Christian Centre approached Rory and me to assist a dear and longstanding friend, Howard Condor, in setting up their television department. We tried every way that we knew how to convince them that they didn't need us, but they wouldn't take no for an answer. So the next and most vital step came into place and we joined the staff at Cornerstone Christian Centre in Bromley, Kent.

I had already sensed that Rory needed deliverance from generational curses, especially that of Freemasonry. I had known, but had taken lightly, the fact that both his father figures, Stan Perrins (step) and Bob Stephen (natural) were very active Freemasons as their fathers had been before them.

But God was about to reveal, through a precious and discerning couple, that Freemasonry had a legal and watertight stranglehold over Rory's heart and mind because of unbroken generational curses.

Whilst the tours were going on, God had revealed to me that Rory was spiritually deaf, blind and hard of heart and that there had been a blockage to his spiritual growth for years. What we later discovered was that the actual vows made during the indoctrination of freemasonry involved placing a black bag over the head (spiritually blind and deaf) and putting a knife to the heart.

This same couple prayed for Rory and he was set free in a manner that was truly remarkable. But this was only the beginning of his Damascus experience.

Now, the only problem seemed to be that we were now placed on a meagre ministry salary which barely covered our mortgage. We found ourselves going backwards financially without making any inroads on the Shakatak debt.

It was during this time on the staff at Cornerstone that Rory, as any good producer would do, started to look for an outlet for the Christian programmes that we were making at the church. On this basis, he started to meet and connect with many of the people in England who were then involved in trying to launch Christian television.

First, it was a total shock to realise that there was literally *no* daily Christian television in Europe. Second, everyone we met said that it was an *impossible* task. *Then*, we heard that even those with all the money and the power had also been unable to launch.

Well, that was all well and good, we were just looking for an outlet for the church programmes. We still viewed Christian television with some suspicion as being ghettoised and not reaching out to a dying and lost world.

But during this period, Rory woke up with a strong conviction: 'Launch Christian television into Europe.'

We both looked at each other. There were literally *dozens* of people everywhere trying desperately to launch Christian television. Some of them had been trying for *years*! Why should we succeed where so very many others had failed? We daren't just move ahead on a good idea. We had to be *sure* that this was God.

But the conviction continued to grow until after several weeks of prayer and time spent before the Lord, we were convinced.

Rory had already investigated the possibility of putting the church programme on the local cable company Nynex, and began to meet with some of the cable operators. During one secular meeting with several channel representatives, he met

Lawrence Nugent, Managing Director of the Black Identity Channel, known as BET International—now closed down.

Rory and Lawrence struck up an immediate affinity and a relationship started to develop. Rory started to explore the possibility of placing Christian programming on BET each Sunday morning. Finally, after Rory's persistent persuasion the first Christian programming *ever shown* on cable in London was placed on BETI.

Where God anoints, He opens the way. Rory has an apostolic call to the media on his life. When there is an apostolic call, there is a bulldozing, a spearheading, a breaking through of new ground. God will confirm His word and His callings with signs and wonders, so Rory and I *expect* signs and wonders in the media.

And we sensed that God indeed would use this anointing to open up the secular television channel, BET International, to the gospel. And that is *exactly* what God did.

The second minister that Rory placed on BETI was Dr Fred Price of Crenshaw Christian Centre, Los Angeles. Then came Creflo Dollar and Carlton Pearson in quick succession, and a whole block of three-hourly ministries to be on once a week on the Black Identity Channel.

It was during this same period, however, that we met with Paul Cowdery, Dr Morris Cerullo's European Director. For many complex reasons, their European Family network had at that time failed to launch and Paul felt that we should meet with Dr Cerullo.

We were summoned in great anticipation to Grosvenor House, where we proceeded to share the vision that God had given us for the Christian Channel Europe with the man himself.

Dr Cerullo viewed us politely and with curiosity. He listened to these two young people and their envisioned presentation very patiently. Then he laid down his conditions. If any agreement was ever to be made, it would mean that he would own the channel but that we would have the security of salaries and every assistance ever needed. He also suggested to Rory that he fly out and meet with David Cerullo, his son.

We explained that we were not looking at this primarily as a commercial venture, but rather as a ministry with a commercial foundation, for God had specifically spoken to us and said that no one ministry or investor could control the channel. We would need to have creative and spiritual control over the decisions of the channel or the vision could possibly be distorted.

Dr Cerullo smiled slowly (and I must add, with great compassion) and said, 'In that case, you'll have to tough it out.'

Rory nodded. He had been given a direct mandate from the Lord never to sell our birthright no matter how much material security or prestige was offered to us.

But *hysterical coward* named Wendy seated next to him, on the other hand, having just discovered that she was pregnant with our second baby and with the mortgage payment looming near, was tempted to clutch Dr Cerullo's hand in desperation and say, 'Yes, yes, I'll sign it . . . Give me the papers . . . NOW!'

By this stage, I would have quite heartily have signed our life away for a 'bowl of soup' and the sooner the better. We needed security. We needed infrastructure. We needed *capital*!

But of course, all I did, apart from a moment when my teeth almost bit through my top lip, was to smile sweetly, (if with extreme pallor, which I'm sure was excused as morning sickness!) as Rory earnestly said . . . 'In that case, Dr Cerullo . . . ', there was a brief hesitation, ' . . . we'll tough it out, sir.'

And needless to say, the heat started to blister through the desolate wasteland of launching Christian television wherein we wandered . . . and with that brave sentence ringing in our ears, we left the sumptuous luxury of Grosvenor House, Mayfair and drove back in stunned silence to our humbler abode in East Molesey, Surrey.

Chapter Five

❖ ❖ ❖

A New Man

*B*y now, we had met a small group of Christian businessmen who were excited about the vision. After much discussion and prayer, we all concluded that the best manner in which to achieve independence was to raise the money ourselves to finance Christian television.

Enter Ishmael . . . in the form of GOLD.

First, from South Africa came an opportunity via Rory's father who was in the publishing business. One of the publications he represented was called *Mining Journal*. He had been approached by a small gold dealer in Ghana to export gold to Europe for which a seemly profit could be made. A *very* seemly profit.

Aha! All eyes lit up (especially as so many Christian businessmen in the UK that we had met at that time were by all accounts bankrupt or rapidly progressing that way) . . . this must be God's provision . . . *a gold deal*!

And so, the dastardly deal progressed.

Rory flew out to Ghana to see how the land lay. But God had a different plan in store for him. The morning after his arrival, he was woken at the crack of dawn by a young black gentleman called Stephen.

Stephen was to arrange a meeting between Rory and Mr Philip Amoaku, a goverment official and the number two in the Geological Survey Department. Philip also happened to be Stephen's older brother.

Sitting on the veranda of this one-star hotel, Rory felt led to tell Stephen that the reason that he was in Ghana and interested in gold exports was because he was a born-again Christian and wanted to make healthy profits in order to fund Christian television in Europe.

Stephen's face lit up, exclaiming that he too was born again!

Rory and Stephen ended up having four hours of private church that morning. Rory sat, aghast at the wisdom of the Holy Spirit pouring from this young man, as he quoted scripture after scripture, hour after hour, without a Bible in sight.

Stephen met with Rory again the next morning, with the Holy Spirit once again moving profoundly through this young account- ant. Then Stephen announced that his older brother, Philip, would meet Rory on Tuesday.

During this time the gold dealer was stalling on Rory, claiming that before negotiations could proceed, Rory would have to meet the Chief of this particular tribe who were trying to sell their gold output.

Rory arrived with Stephen at the governmental offices in Accra to meet Philip. Well, compared to the godly Philip, Stephen was but a spiritual *babe*!

'The Man of God said you would come,' said Philip.

Rory looked at him questioningly.

'Two years ago, he told us a white man would come who would bring Christian television to Europe. He knows you are coming and now you are here.'

Rory's eyes nearly fell out. 'I will tell him you are here,' continued Philip.

At this point, the gold deal started to pale into insignificance as God's greater plan and His sovereign purpose started to manifest themselves.

Rory dutifully met the persons involved in the exporting of the gold, looked over their operation and requested more detailed paperwork and their government credentials before Philip appeared.

'The Man of God will meet with you. God has said he must pray for you!'

Now by this time, it had become very evident to Rory that Prophet Kwame, as he was called, was no ordinary pastor.

In the next few days, whenever he had free time after finishing his business with the gold company, he would spend his leisure time with a growing group of the 'Man of God's' disciples. They were all the same. They radiated the glory and the power of God.

Rory started to learn more about Prophet Kwame. He had been a sinner and one night, the Lord Jesus had appeared to him personally and his whole life had been transformed. There were stories of miracles and talk of 'the fear of God descending', so much so that the night before Rory was to meet him, he became exceptionally uneasy.

Rory phoned me from Accra to say that he really felt that he should stay to meet with him and I just knew by the sound in his voice that something profound was taking place.

God was preparing to clean up any left-over residue from Rory's old life and a supernatural impartation was about to take place that would mean Rory Alec would never be the same man again.

Well, dear readers, I received my husband back a *new* man. Not a *changed* man . . . but a *new* man. It was as though Rory had been born again for the first time. How can I describe it? When he walked in, the fear of God started to descend on me. There was an awesomeness involved in what had taken place in Rory's life and it was evident to all. He was transformed. A supernatural fire now burned in him for God.

And so, for the first time since I had been married to Rory, I stood in awe as I sensed a call of God on his life so *strong* that I *knew* this was the same kind of call that had operated over other apostolic men that God had raised up to fulfil His purposes.

There had been an impartation that had released the fullness of an apostolic anointing to shake the foundations of Satan's previously held media bastions. But more than that, there was now in evidence a call to the fivefold ministry, an anointing that would grow with the months as a fire to preach the gospel, as God had intended for him since the beginning of time.

God never leads without equipping. We often hear the cliché, 'Where God guides, He provides' and indeed God had by a powerful, sovereign impartation through the Holy Ghost started to equip Rory for the mammoth apostolic work that would lie ahead.

I knew that from that point onward he would never be the same, and he never has. And that, dear readers, is the greatest miracle of all.

Chapter Six

❖ ❖ ❖

A Prophet on Time

*R*ory was now an associate minister of Cornerstone Christian Centre. We were working very hard to develop the television department there and after a brief discussion, and with much wisdom on their part, the pastors acknowledged that God was indeed separating us out for the sake of the gospel and the calling on our lives. (We would eventually resign from being staff members a few months later with their full blessing and encouragement.)

At the end of July, our church was involved in a prophetic convention and we attended the Friday as part of the staff. We had never been the kind who would run after the prophets. We believed that God was well able to intervene prophetically if He chose, and we were happy to leave prophetic confirmations in His hands.

But something different stirred in our hearts that Friday. We watched as this Malaysian prophet started to move under the prophetic anointing.

This anointing was *so* accurate and *so* profound that together, without knowing it, Rory and I both sensed that God would speak and confirm His call on our lives through His prophet. The meeting came and ended but there was no word for us.

It was my father's birthday on the Saturday, so we could not attend the next day's meetings. We walked away, slightly discouraged. Unknowingly, we had *both* felt that God had something for us. But there was nothing to do but to walk hand in hand with God ourselves and continue to take the steps of faith required.

However, when we arrived at church, two Sundays later, who should be preaching in the morning service but Jonathan David. We were seated right in the corner, tucked away out of the camera's reach.

Jonathan David started to preach. Suddenly, about a quarter of the way into his sermon, teaching on the apostolic, break-through church, he hesitated briefly, saying, 'There are people in this place who are going to raise up television networks as never before . . . as never before.'

He reverted back to his sermon, then stopped and asked for those involved in television: he said, 'All those who have this "passion" for television, stand up.' Then, ignoring everyone else, he turned straight to Rory and me tucked away in the corner and pointed his finger directly at us.

He looked at us with the fire of God gleaming in his eyes and started to prophesy. 'God shows me that you are like a stone cut out from a different place. God brought you here that you might become part of what He is doing here, and right across Europe, right across Germany . . . ' (At this stage, we were only looking at cable in England.) The complete prophecy is at the very front of this book, but the most profound thing was that by the end of this prophetic word, Jonathan David was talking specifically about a television network that would turn the destiny of entire churches, a network that would change the destiny of the Church.

This prophecy was given on 31 July 1994 and today in 1996, we watch this prophetic word come to pass *every day*.

God used a prophet from Malaysia, who knew nothing about us, didn't know us from a bar of soap, to say, 'Yes, my children, this is my work, this is MY mandate to you. Be strong and very courageous and run with what I have commanded you that Europe shall be saved.'

And so, we said, 'Yes sir!' And started to run.

As well as working for the church, placing ministries on BET and starting to contact the British cable operators, we attended the 'Believers' Convention' with Kenneth and Gloria Copeland in late August 1994.

Now, of course, we were invincible. We had the assurance that Father God Himself was behind us!

So, we arrived at the Believers' Convention knowing that Kenneth and Gloria were excited about Christian television and sat all through the week completely assured of the fact that surely 'CHRISTIAN TELEVISION EUROPE' simply must be written all over us in the spirit realm. So fired up were we, that like little groupies, we sat for most of the evening in the foyer of the Hyatt Hotel deliberating whether to leave our reams of Christian television proposals for them at the desk, perchance they would read our vision and get excited.

We had to leave on the Friday morning, so on the Thursday evening, unable to restrain ourselves any longer and feeling prompted to get the relevant information to Jesse Duplantis, we 'accosted' Jesse's wife as she followed him out of the auditorium before the end of the service.

'This is for Jesse,' we hissed *sotto volce*.

Anyway, we were fairly disheartened that Kenneth Copeland didn't look over our way and suddenly boom, 'There they are! *These* are the people for Christian television. Come and have dinner.'

And of course, Jesse from stage would just stop and pick us out from among ten thousand people and say, 'I *know* by the Spirit that *you* are the ones who sent me the letter!' Oh Lord, forgive us the vain imaginations!

We left downhearted, only to hear that Kenneth gave a dynamic prophecy about Christian television on the Friday night. That made us even more downhearted that we weren't there! To make matters worse, we then heard that one of the other hundred groups of people trying to launch Christian television had in fact met with John Copeland.

But God found a way through for us and the very next week, Kim Freeborn, European director for Kenneth Copeland Ministries, phoned Pastor Hugh Osgood to ask for further information about us. This led to a meeting with Kim.

We drove to Bath where Kim took us out for what was to be at that stage, a very welcome Chinese dinner. (It must have been very evident to him that we were on our last legs.)

Kim listened very patiently and then kindly offered to give us an appointment with John Copeland when he and Derek Turner, the new International Director, came out on their next trip to England.

You see, the first ministry that God spoke to us to put on in Europe was Kenneth and Gloria Copeland. We knew beyond any doubt that no matter what the opposition, God had said to us 'MY WORD MUST GO FORTH BOLDLY.' In fact, the Copelands were the only ministry, at that stage, that the Holy Spirit instructed us to place on the Christian Channel every day. Rory had already been dealing with Integrity Communications, the Copeland's media buyer, when he had placed Creflo Dollar on the cable channel, BET. So, God placed Peggy Kinner of Integrity, a tough, no-nonsense, very smart businesswoman, in line to hear about the vision of the Christian Channel through Rory.

But at times, we still longed to get past the 'business' fronts of the ministries, believing that when we met Kenneth and Gloria, they would be inspired and excited by the fact that the Christian Channel had been birthed purely by faith; but at that time, it was not to be.

(To complete the story, nearly two years later, we arrived at the 1996 International Believers' Convention on the Tuesday night. Kenneth Copeland came on stage.

'Where are Rory and Wendy Alec?' he demanded, those piercing eagle eyes shining with glee. 'Stand up.'

Brother Kenneth announced the Christian Channel with tremendous excitement and what was so evident was his absolute joy that God had used two young people to launch Christian television into Europe by faith!

Oh, we were so encouraged that night. We knew from friends in Dallas that Kenneth and Gloria had been monitoring our progress through the months. This was a tremendous comfort to us because we knew that if any *two people in the world must have understood all the trials and testings and mountains that had stood in our way through this walk of faith . . . they certainly did.*

Rory was privileged to meet with both Kenneth and Gloria the following evening. Unfortunately I could not be there, but Rory said that when they prayed for him, it was as though the literal sword of the Spirit pierced right through him.

God is faithful to bring His Josephs in front of His Pharaohs for HIS purposes in Europe to be accomplished. How awed we are at God's amazing faithfulness to us.

That same evening, we were sitting in the second row, behind Jesse Duplantis and his wife. Jesse's ministry has been a consistent source of encouragement to the Christian Channel from the time of our launch. One cold, winter's evening in December, Jesse even phoned us on our mobile just to say, 'Thank you' and to encourage us to fight for the faith—truly a word in season.

*So, here at the Believers' Convention, Jesse leaned over
and handed us a cheque for the ministry. Later in the hotel, we
opened it. It was a cheque for ten thousand dollars! Oh, God
bless Jesse and his wife for their generosity and obedience to
the Holy Spirit.*

*Isn't it so wonderful to know that the men and women our
viewers watch every day on screen, live what they preach; that
the life and love of God flow through them as much offscreen as
on. We have been privileged by God to come before many of this
generation's generals and Pharoahs and as much as their giftings
and callings vary, we can say without fail that the
integrity and sincerity displayed by the men and women broadcasting into Europe is without question.)*

Anyway, back to August 1994!

·   We continued to contact the cable operators and they were
intrigued at this new potential subscriber base, but cautious as to
the controversy surrounding Christian programming, particularly
as relating to the American televangelists. Basically one and all
agreed that when we were up and running, they would, more
often than not, carry us, but until then, they could not forward us
the letter of intent we so desperately needed to raise the funds
necessary to launch.

So, at this stage, we return to the gold deal which was still
pending. Rory had met briefly with Dr John Avanzini, a teacher
of biblical economics and he had advised that indeed to
preserve independence, we should try to raise our own money to
launch.

The natural solution was, of course, we concluded—the gold
deal.

Oh, hallelujah—would we never learn that God wanted all
the glory out of launching Christian television in Europe, not to
give it to a group of Christian businessmen or to a good deal that
Rory made? But of course, the brick wall was looming up again.

By this time, we had resigned from Cornerstone Christian Centre and I was eight months pregnant.

Calls to and from Ghana were now generated in a flurry. The refinery was set up here to receive the gold. Then it would be sold onto the open market in London.

Everybody was working intensively on this deal. Contractually, it would mean that for twelve months, we would receive a shipment of unrefined gold at Heathrow and resell it onto the open market, making an excellent profit of which our share would be enough to run the then cable channel for a year.

This we felt was a really comfortable arrangement. Well, the lawyers and accountants had started to set things up. And Rory's father was even flying in from Johannesburg to spend a night here and then do the final groundwork in Accra.

I should mention, that during this time, on the second of December, I delivered our gorgeous sunny second baby called Christian Alec. The consultant advised another caesarean as he warned that this was likely to be a large baby. Christian weighed in at ten pounds and four ounces.

Straight after the birth I haemorrhaged badly. After the nurse's initial panic, I was settled in the emergency room. My parents and Rory left. Well—there I was, still in the emergency room, *sans* make up, looking as if I had been dragged in from the African bush, when suddenly in burst three excited men with 'goldfever' written all over their brows: Rory, his father, Bob Stephen and a colleague.

I was handed a few bunches of wilted hospital flowers, some strange sort of daisy which looked as if they had seen better days, and the conversation that night in the emergency room seemed to centre more on the gold than that we actually had a new son. (I am being cruel!)

And here comes Hollywood, guys. The Ghanaian gold dealer gave them a kilogram of gold dust as security. Nine thousand dollars was paid to allow the release of the container onto the plane which never did take place! Five days later, the gold was tested and it disintegrated . . . it *was* fake! Nearly nine months' work in ashes . . . and naturally, the dealer disappeared off the face of the planet . . . with *our* dollars.

Well now, there was a Proverbs 31 wife with our one-week-old baby, acting strangely like another wife in a certain more unflattering section of Proverbs! Both Rory and I had resigned from the church, our commission from Christian Media Placements would only be paid to us at the end of January . . . do you know, dear readers, we had *twenty pounds* over Christmas!

Now we had been through hard times before and when we first arrived in England, there were times we didn't have groceries in our cupboard, and I couldn't buy Sam clothes, but this was it!

We slunk down to my parents with not even enough money for presents, Rory looking slightly pale every time my mother asked him about the progression of the gold deal. When my brother, the budding doctor, and his wife came on Boxing Day, that was the final nail in the coffin. Now we not only felt like the poor relations—we *were* the poor relations!

My father, who has me completely taped, would look at me suspiciously and mutter, just within ear shot, remarks inferring that he thought 'born again Christians' were supposed to be radiant, not to go about his house scowling darkly!

And so we made our way back up to Surrey, with nothing to come back to in the natural. The dream was completely dashed, the cupboards were bare, the baby that I had vowed would have everything seemed to have been born into a worse state than Samantha. My stitches were still sore, but as I worshipped my Father God, there was a deep assurance that all would be well and in His hands. We took the most rational and sensible step and, dear readers, we went on income support.

God in His infinite wisdom allowed us to go through many things.

Rory and I know what it's like to live the high life, but we also know what it's like for thousands out there who are on income support on a tiny income. We know what it's like to fail and to hardly have enough to clothe the children. Friends, I know what it is like not to be able to buy the baby new clothes. I know how it feels to be cooped up day after day with a tiny one not knowing if life will ever change. Oh precious people—if our wonderful Father God can bring us through—He can bring *you* through too.

Chapter Seven

❖ ❖ ❖

Astra

*S*o, there we were, at the beginning of January 1995, with the prophetic word that God would launch a Christian television network, but with all our dreams in tatters. Then, in the second week of the new year, Rory woke up and said, 'God wants us to go for Astra.'

'*Astra!*' I exclaimed, interpreted as, 'Have you finally gone *completely* insane?'

The Astra satellite system was the most highly sought-after satellite system in Europe. The Astra satellite currently beams it's signal into over twenty-two million homes across Europe (four and a half million of those in the UK), a potential sixty-five million people across twenty-four nations. Every significant television channel was on this satellite and we knew beyond any doubt that in the natural, it was completely impossible to gain access on Astra. We had been regaled with stories of how the most powerful ministries and groups of

Christians had tried to get access to the Astra system with absolutely no success.

Eventually Dr Morris Cerullo managed to get a foot in the door with his European Family Network, but this too, did not come to fruition. And now, after months of negotiating with different cable operators, and still not having a definite offer of carriage, the thought of going through months of trying to access this most prized satellite system was almost soul-destroying.

But I *knew* that God had spoken to my husband and we were in the position where either Rory would have to go and get a job in the secular media, or we would choose to pay the price required and follow God's call.

It was the first week of 1995, we had a three-year-old little girl and a four-week-old baby boy. We were faced with a dashed gold deal, cable operators who were sitting on the fence and not even a glimmer of light in our future.

But deep inside both of us, there was still something that whispered, 'Fight . . . don't give up . . . don't give up now.'

Rory phoned Astra's headquarters. They were not the slightest bit interested to hear about Christian television. He spoke to our media legal consultants, who said it was impossible. Ministries we were in contact with, said: 'Impossible—we've tried, can't be done.' *Every* place we turned to for wisdom and advice stated quite categorically that accessing the Astra satellite system was the ultimate impossibility.

But the requirement necessary to break through Satan's iron grip on the media, and specifically the Astra satellite, was the anointing to fulfil the task. And yes, many had gone before us, but this is where God's prophetic destiny for us as individuals was about to run its course.

God required new wine for a new wineskin. He was not going to allow old wine that had been used to spearhead Christian television into other parts of the world to simply transplant to Europe, because He had a brand new and unique agenda for Europe.

And deep in our hearts, we began to sense that the reason that there had been so many casualties in Europe was because what was required to open up the gates to Christian television in dark, stiff-necked Europe would be the Living God's apostolic anointing to media.

The apostolic is a breakthrough, foundational anointing . . . an anointing that would be able to confront the strongholds of darkness over the continent of Europe and boldly challenge the Prince of the Power of the airwaves.

But without that breakthrough anointing, we believe, many dear, well-meaning people were hurt and wounded in their heroic attempts to launch Christian television into Europe.

God had also equipped us with the gift of faith and with this gift comes a tremendous boldness to opposition and impossibility. He also knew that we would not just produce a channel that was to be a 'bless me' club, for the apostolic encompasses all elements of the fivefold ministry. This channel was to teach and preach, to evangelise, to pastor and to impact Europe prophetically. The Christian Channel would herald in REVIVAL.

Another result of an apostolic call to the media is that it will affect the secular media. And that was the second requirement that God had for His launching of Christian television—that it was to be a sign and a wonder in the midst of an unbelieving generation. I have stated earlier that often Christian projects that Rory and I were involved intended to attract attention in the secular press, and so, God once again would confirm His call and His anointing for His mighty endtime purpose in Europe.

Later, when many were saying, 'You came out of nowhere' and the ones who had been faithfully working at Christian television for years were calling us 'young upstarts', we knew that it was no mistake or accident that Europe had remained closed for a specific time.

God's attention is riveted on Europe and the part it will play in these endtimes. The coming revival in Europe is a revival that will sweep the nations of the earth. And God has a timetable, and His timetable cannot be pushed forward by man.

And so, a hundredfold thanks to all those who have faithfully prayed for Christian television, and what a great debt is owed to each one of God's faithful intercessors, for indeed it is the intercessors that clear the way for God's chosen warriors to fight the battle.

God's chosen, appointed vessels may not, to the natural eye, be the most established or the most learned . . . but as young David went out to face Goliath in God's ordained battle plan, so I believe that we were sent out by the Living God to literally demolish the jeering Goliath here in Europe which continually taunted with, 'Where is your God amongst all this filth and adultery and pornography and violence? Where is this God that so many of you in the UK and Europe say you serve?'

And now, Christians across Europe can *boldly* rise up and shout: 'Here is the sign and the wonder in the midst of a perverse and unbelieving generation—here is God's sign across Europe—that the iron curtain of the media in Satan's kingdom will never again be the same as it was before the first of October 1995.'

But we will devote a chapter to the cynical press later, now back to Astra. Rory contacted the leaseholders on the Astra satellite. Three came back to us for discussion. And the biggest miracle of all was the fact that one of them was no less than BSkyB— jointly owned by Rupert Murdoch.

Sky were prepared to enter into preliminary negotiations with us and furnish us with a letter of intent on condition that we received our ITC licence (a licence to broadcast courtesy of the Independent Television Commission).

But the same week that BSkyB came through—a major catastrophe struck. I had a breast cancer scare.

Well, that was it. Now, completely paranoid, it became

evident to me that the devil's plan was very obvious. He had been waiting for me to go through all the suffering of hardship and poverty and heartache, just to kill me when the dream was about to come true.

I finally got it—now I was going to die. That was it—the devil's final annihilation of Wendy Alec. Out in a flash. One foul swoop.

I wish you could have seen this woman of faith and valour . . . because she was a gibbering wreck. In the week leading up to the ultrasound, I lost twelve pounds. (I didn't keep them off long!)

I proceeded to drive my family and friends (Annie, my age-old friend, had come over from Malawi) completely up the wall with my deteriorating behaviour.

Finally the ultrasound came and went and the results were clear.

Now, let me take a more serious tone.

Friends, you never know what you believe until you are tested. It is the easiest thing to recite glib words of faith for healing but the *only* time that you will *truly* know what you believe is when *you* are put in that ultimate test yourself.

So, here we have a doctor's daughter who had never been sick in her life. I had never had a desire to pray for the sick; I would always pass them onto someone who was anointed in that area. I never had a true compassion for the sick; instead I would think, 'Just stand on the Word and get healed.'

If I ever was sick with only very minor ailments, my father always had the answer and the medication to heal me, so I *never* had to look to God in this area.

And then, for the first time in my life, I was confronted with what could have been a life-or-death situation . . . and I discovered I had no faith. Here was this 'faith' person, a Rhema Bible School graduate, and I had *no* faith.

I was a demented, sobbing wreck, preparing to leave my baby

and family, my creative, dramatic imagination knowing no bounds . . . it was funeral time.

This was just the beginning.

Briefly, the next thing that happened was that I started to cough and had a strange virus in my chest, on the same side right next door to the dubious area. Then, at the same time, the symptoms worsened and I was told by my encouraging younger brother (the new doctor) that the ultrasound could have missed something. Also, I had severe shooting pains reaching to under my arm. It all came together to make a terrifying picture.

Now, of course, I was under a consultant in the National Health system. Well, during the next two months, the symptoms worsened and then it was time for our first trip to America . . . Finally, on our arrival back from America, they decided to book me in for a mammogram. Meanwhile, I had started to read and recite healing scriptures, but every night, without fail, I would be gripped by absolute terror as soon as the darkness came, no matter how much I prayed.

You see, what had actually happened in the spirit realm was that I had become so affected by fear in January, that I had allowed a spirit of fear to oppress me . . . and it surely was.

Well, the mammogram was clear. The searing pain was attributed to a disturbance in the lymphatic system. The peripheral symptoms were, 'they' said, something I would have to live with after the baby . . . and the frightening ongoing chest pain was labelled an ongoing virus. I was delirious with joy. *Finally*, I had been given the all clear.

Ten days later, I was knocked off my feet by a nausea that was so severe that I would almost faint with it. My head would swim, I could hardly stand, and the most terrifying aspect was this overwhelming weakness.

Six weeks later, this was still going on. At times I could hardly walk. I was transferred to a consultant. I was lined up for all kinds of tests. There was a CAT scan, a gastroscopy and blood test after blood test.

To cut a long story short, these debilitating attacks continued on and off for nine months. During the terror of this year, and by fighting and fighting against the fear of this unknown terrible illness, I not only became strong in my faith, but I developed a supreme hatred of the spirit of infirmity and the spirit of disease and death. I came to an understanding that with victory comes authority. God has used these circumstances to give me a profound compassion for the sick and with it, a healing anointing has started to manifest itself through my life, totally by His grace. I give our wonderful great Healer all the glory.

Chapter Eight

❖ ❖ ❖

The American Dream

Well, now we had to impress the Independent Television Commission.

It had taken another Christian organisation up to eighteen months to obtain their ITC licence, and by all accounts in the natural, we could once again be on the verge of a very long haul.

Apart from that, we needed credibility. We needed lawyers and accountants and large bank accounts and religious organisations. So we looked around to marshal anyone and everyone around us who seemed to fit the category.

By the end of our paperwork, our company secretary was a Jewish firm of Trustees who handled millions of pounds' worth of pension funds each month in an offshore account. Our lawyers were the prestigious Simpkins (one of the most reputable set of media lawyers in London), among other strategically placed and credible names.

Then came a call from the ITC, brushing all of the pomp and

ceremony aside and saying, 'No, no—we want to know about Rory and Wendy Alec.'

Well, our hearts in the natural were in our boots; this was like literally taking little David and bringing him before Saul to study his credentials. Other soldiers would have had a list as long as their arm of strategic battles, winning medals for service and for valour, and on David's application there would just have been: 'Fought a lion. Fought a bear.'

And so we filled in our lion and bear application and waited with bated breath.

It was now the beginning of March. We had also, at the same time, remortgaged our house to pay off some of the lawyers' and accountants' bills and to enable us to survive.

Rory was booked to travel to Amsterdam to share the vision with a group of Christians working in the media in Europe, set up by Bert Panhuis who organised the occasion.

On the Wednesday that he was to speak in Amsterdam, our ITC licence application was taken to board level (because it was a religious licence) and the decision as to whether or not Rory and Wendy Alec could launch a religious channel across the United Kingdom and Europe was to be taken. (Strongly imprinted on our minds was the length of time it had taken the other religious licence holder to get approval.) Rory arrived and was confronted by approximately fifty curious and some unsmiling, severe faces.

There were those who were excited about the vision, but then again there were those who had themselves been involved in Christian media for years and viewed Rory and me as not only young upstarts, but as downright arrogant—to think that 'we' could dare succeed where so many older, more experienced people, who had been faithful for years, had failed.

Everything hinged on the decision that afternoon. If we didn't get our ITC Licence, we had no Christian Channel and no deal with BSkyB.

So there was Rory in Amsterdam and me down in the New Forest in Dorset, with my parents and the children, and our whole destiny hinged in the natural on the ITC board's decision.

Rory arrived back home, after his sharing of the vision followed by interrogation by some of the sceptics in Europe, feeling rather flat. He started to thumb through the pile of post waiting for him at home (mostly bills).

Well, there at the bottom of the pile was a largish envelope that was stamped by the ITC.

Rory picked it up. Later he admitted that he started to brace himself for the long haul that everyone was expecting to be the next step, with all kinds of appeals for information pertaining to ourselves and the channel—the beginning of a logistical nightmare.

Well, dear friends, our God is a *wonder-working, miracle-working* God, for there in the envelope was a letter that stated 'We are pleased to award the Christian Channel Europe a licence from the Independent Broadcasting Commission to broadcast for ten years.'

Our secular media lawyers, who dealt with these applications as a matter of course, said that they had never seen an application processed so quickly. They said that they must have literally got up from the board meeting on the Thursday and processed the licence to arrive in the post by Saturday morning. Where God guides, He indeed provides!

Needless to say there was much rejoicing in the New Forest on Rory's arrival and now, it was time to take a trip to the 'land of milk and honey' . . . America—here we come!

By this time, all our funds were depleted with lawyers' and accountants' fees, with telephone bills to the States and living expenses, but there was still an inner sensing that we *must* take this trip.

A week before we were supposed to leave, we were at a church in Brussels and a prophetic word was spoken over us by a visiting American speaker that we would be travelling within ten days and would receive great favour with men. Well, immediately we put two and two together. 'Great favour' equals money.

To cut a long story short, the day before we left, no funds had come through. Then a certain pastor, with a church in Europe, said he knew we *had* to go and therefore he was prepared to cover the credit card expenses (of a fourth party travelling with us) in the unlikely event that we raised no money.

You see, this was now subtly turning into the 'money' trip. We were totally convinced that as soon as America heard the vision of the Christian Channel and knew that we had a firm offer from BSkyB and an ITC licence, that the thousands would come pouring in. In fact the hundreds of thousands!

So, we left, in great faith, with total assurance that *this* was the trip to raise the funds necessary to launch the Christian Channel. Welcome America—first stop Chicago, to meet with Jerry Rose, founder of WCFC Chicago.

Well, we sat with Jerry and his right-hand man, Dave and enthusiastically shared the vision. What we didn't know at that stage, was that America had been literally wrung dry with well-meaning people attempting to raise funds and support for their dreams of Christian television in Europe. And of course, none of these ventures had ever seen the light of day.

Now, let me say here that Jerry and Dave were extremely personable and I think that Jerry himself identified with us, thinking back to his own initial years of struggle, but we left the next day with basically a pat on the head and a smile.

The next stop was off to Marion, Illinois to meet with Garth Kuns and his wife.

Well, Garth seemed slightly more disinterested than Jerry, but again he and his wife were very charming. Our vision just didn't seem to touch a chord in them.

Well, after a flurry of phone calls made from an American

motel, we finally managed to get an appointment to meet with
Paul Crouch (founder of Trinity Broadcasting Network) in
Nashville. We had previously been in touch with Terence Hickey,
his executive assistant.

We were taken to the dressing rooms after the live presentation of 'Praise the Lord' where we met for about twenty minutes
with Paul Crouch.

He again, was extremely courteous and asked for a proposal,
but we sensed that he too had met so many previous Christian
television Europe enthusiasts that he probably looked at the
vision of this young couple and placed it on the shelf to see if it
would come to pass.

We were learning fast.

It seemed that in America until your vision was established,
there would be a reluctance to assist in any concrete way.

We had come over believing that *this* was the nation that
operated by faith, *these* were the visionaries, only to
discover that there seemed to be a tremendous reserve towards
any vision that wasn't already tangible.

This was becoming hard for all of us to understand. God was
vitally interested in Europe, but Europe didn't have a vision or
understanding of Christian Television. Was *no one* going to see
the tremendous mission field that could be reached through
Christian television?   Was everyone *only* interested in the
commercial aspect of what they got out of it? Did no one think
souls any more? Had they all *forgotten* that they too had started
by faith? Would *everyone* insist on controlling the vision?

What we later learned was that many, many well-meaning
people, among them several opportunists, had approached these
people that *we* were now approaching. In fact they had been
approached to get behind Christian television in every obscure
part of the world, and hardly any of these visions had actually
come to fruition. So of course, when we came along all fuelled
up with *vision* and *passion*, they had seen it all before.

'But we are *different*!' we exclaimed.

And they would all smile patiently and nod, saying, 'Keep us updated on your progress. God bless you.' And with a shake of the hand, they would be gone.

Each meeting became more disillusioning, and slowly we were becoming discouraged.

It became evident that no one in America was going to support us until we actually launched; that the *only* thing that would convince America of our credibility was not, as we had hoped, the firm offer from Sky and our ITC licence, but the actual *existence* of the channel.

Oh where were the men and woman of faith and vision, who would be prepared to step out on the water with us? But you see, dear reader, God was putting us through *His* school.

However, I have to tell you, the fire of God in Rory and me could not be extinguished. They could ignore us, they could tell us we would end up like other casualties of Christian television, but *no one* would be able to extinguish the flame of the Christian Channel Europe, simply because *this* vision *was* birthed of God Himself.

We continued on our journey up towards Dallas and stopped in Houston, where we were promised five minutes with Pastor John Osteen, after the evening service.

Well, we all went back to his office where we proceeded to give an impassioned account of what God wanted us to do in Europe. So there we were, in mid flow, eyes ablaze with vision, when suddenly Pastor John got to his feet, stretched, yawned and said, 'These old bones are tired. Goodnight.' (We had not realised he had promised us literally just five minutes!)

And so we were left, facing Dodie, with shock obviously registered all over our faces. Dodie very graciously showed us through the offices, but we must admit that we left that evening with the distinct feeling that at the end of the day, it was just going to be us and God.

However, we left it in the Father's hands, and so gracious

was He, because when Rory arrived the following morning to spend time with Joel Osteen, who should Rory bump into but Pastor John Osteen himself, now remarkably refreshed from the evening's rest. Rory actually spent the good part of an hour with him as he showed him around the building. So, God had His way!

But there were still no funds raised. Not one American cent.

Next stop Dallas, to visit with Marcus and Joni Lamb. And here, there was an affinity. We shared the vision on their programme and people started ringing. Marcus and Joni, a generous-hearted, visionary couple, were also excited and it was to be a divine connection that God would pick up later. The next morning we were to have a very interesting meeting . . .

We arrived at a church in Dallas just as an incredibly smooth, well-oiled-looking gentleman climbed out of his gleaming new Jaguar. Not a hair was out of place, his trousers creased to the max . . . here in front of us was this semi-charismatic legend in person, staring at us, I might add, with a vague curiosity.

He showed us round his new television studio and then proceeded to take us into a private room. He looked at us with an even vaguer curiosity which continued all through our presentation of the vision, (which was remarkably less impassioned, now that we had been battered by the winds of American scepticism).

The above-mentioned gentleman saw immediately that the desperate, overriding need was, of course, financial. And here, I must say, all credit to him, he immediately said, 'Let's pray and see what God says.'

And here it started. Immediately, he started to groan. But dear reader, I mean . . . GR . . . OA . . . OA . . . N.

All our eyes were on stalks, all staring at him together, until we remembered our manners and closed them rapidly. He continued to groan remarkably loudly. But this time we were each just opening *one* eye, at intervals, staring like John Cleese.

'You've got to GROAN . . . REALLY GR . . . OA . . . OA . . . N', he commanded us.

And so, we *all* started to groan in a more suitable manner.

After several minutes (it seemed more like an hour), he furrowed his brows. His eyes were closed tightly.

'I sense God has given me a figure . . . He's saying . . . '

We all leaned forward in anticipation.

'The figure is . . . ' Another long, drawn-out groan.

Our leaning now was stretched to the limit as we waited with bated breath (this had in the past been an extremely cash-rich ministry until the scandal which shook it to its foundations).

Now, all of us, great propagators of 'God is our source', suddenly looked disgustingly interested in this figure.

'I've almost got it . . . '

We stared goggle-eyed, looking remarkably like the leaning tower of Pisa, just waiting for the looming figure.

'I've *got* it!'

We all opened our eyes as he looked up suddenly in triumph.

'It's five thousand!'

We all nearly fell backwards.

Oh Father, forgive my sense of the ridiculous, but the thought that immediately flashed through my mind was that with all that remarkable groaning, the figure would have been at least fifty thousand. (But unfortunately when the rubber hit the road, this gentleman reneged on the five thousand dollars.)

And so there we were, standing at the airport about to fly home, discouraged and disillusioned with nothing to show from our grand trip to America but a debt of ten thousand pounds.

Oh *where* was the great favour that we had been convinced we would find with these men? And where was the funding?

But you see, dear reader, our wonderful heavenly Father had allowed us to realise at an early stage of the vision, that for all our lip service as to God being our source, it was very evident that we had subtly started to shift our eyes onto men.

We arrived back from the land of milk and honey tired and, I have to admit, almost shell-shocked. We had gone out in such high hope, with such expectation that God would achieve His miracle to launch the Christian Channel, and to all intents and purposes, it was a trip that had not only seemingly failed in its purpose but we had now discovered, as do all of God's pioneering eagles . . . we were flying alone.

It was a valuable lesson that we would never forget.

Chapter Nine

❖ ❖ ❖

BSkyB

We were now in an interesting situation. We had put off signing with BSkyB, believing that the money we needed as a deposit would have been raised in America. However, this had not come to fruition.

Now, we were faced with a dilemma. *Should* we sign the contract without a brass farthing in the Christian Channel bank account or *should* we wait until the money was forthcoming?

Our secular media lawyers advised us in strong terms that to sign with no money could be seen as fraudulent. But there was a strong feeling inside our spirit that kept urging us, 'Sign, Sign.'

We were waiting every day for BSkyB to carry out a credit check on the Christian Channel, and to demand at least a fifty-thousand deposit when we signed.

But the days passed and there was no credit check and no

request for a deposit. Even our media lawyers shook their heads in wonder and amazement.

Well, the date was set to sign with the General Manager of BSkyB on 14 June 1995.

Friend, you cannot imagine the magnitude of that event to the Christian Channel. Our enemies, the sceptics, were indeed lined up against us. 'They will never launch,' was the devil's taunt.

But we determined not to be discouraged and set our faces like flint. You see, in the Word of God there had been a taunting just as intimidating when David faced Goliath.

> And the Philistine said to David, 'Come to me, and I will give your flesh to the birds of the air and the beasts of the field!'
>
> *1 Samuel 17:44*

And the devil taunted *us* saying, 'Everything's going to come crashing down around you, no airtime, no reputation, no television channel—everything will be destroyed. And you will be the laughing stock of all the sceptics and the British media.'

> Then David said to the Philistine, 'You come to me with a sword, with a spear, and with a javelin. But I come to you in the name of the LORD of Hosts, the God of the armies of Israel, whom you have defied. This day the LORD will deliver you into my hand, and I will strike you and take your head from you. And this day I will give your carcasses of the camp of the Philistines to the birds of the air and the wild beasts of the earth, that all the earth may know that there is a God in Israel. Then all this assembly shall know that the LORD does not save with sword and spear; for the battle is the LORD's and He will give you into our hands.'
>
> *1 Samuel 17:45–47*

And so, we turned to the Goliath of the media in Europe and we said, 'This day the Lord will deliver Sky into our hand. We have been called to this from the beginning of time. This is not just a whim. This is not our idea, but it is the mandate for Rory and Wendy Alec from the Living God that the Christian Channel shall be placed as a sign in the midst of a perverse and unbelieving generation, that Europe may know that there is a God in Israel, that there is a God in Europe.

'Then all the sceptics in Europe and America shall know that the Lord does not save with sword and spear (with money and power) but the battle is the Lord's and He will give the media into our hands.'

With the sound of battle ringing in our ears, we decided that the time had come to sign with BSkyB.

And so, the following week, we made our way over to Osterley. You cannot imagine, dear reader, the exhilaration, the absolute awesomeness of finally walking into Sky to 'possess the land'.

Chris Mackenzie, BSkyB's general manager, was standing looking at us with a slight frown. He then turned to his legal advisor.

'Is everything in order, then?' he asked.

A deathly hush descended on Rory and me and the small group of faithful Christian Channel supporters that had accompanied us. At this point, *our* legal advisors, who could not be there in person, were on the other phone.

We waited with baited breath, the great faith people trembling in their boots in case Chris Mackenzie decided at the last moment to ask for a deposit of 50,000 pounds or we were suddenly asked to produce the dreaded credit reference. Chris Mackenzie frowned. 'Is everything in order?'

The legal gentleman nodded studiedly. All eyes were now glued onto the piece of paper with the vacant signature.

Slowly, Mr Mackenzie picked up the pen and signed the

document. He passed it over to Rory.

'I wish this was a cheque!' he quipped.

Rory signed all the papers enthusiastically.

'So do I,' said Rory.

Chris Mackenzie started and the ruddiness drained from his face, but he caught himself, turned, smiled, shook our hands and informed us that Rupert Murdoch was *not,* as many would believe, without any religious convictions, but was endowed with some finer Catholic sentiments.

This cheered us up. Maybe Rupert Murdoch would watch the Christian Channel secretly in the early hours of morning and become an enthusiastic supporter. Ah! Of such stuff dreams are made. If he becomes an ACTT* supporter, we shall let you all know!

But the deal was done. The contract was signed and we walked out praising and worshipping the living God.

We now we had a watertight agreement with BSkyB. We had our licence (a ten-year licence) from the Independent Television Commission. We had been obedient to the prompting of the Holy Spirit and signed the contract. And within a short time period, we were to discover *why* we had felt the urgency to sign.

A few days later, we received a telephone call from BSkyB, informing us that now that we had a signed contract, they needed one of our hours back . . . *urgently.*

Now originally, we had signed for the hours 7.00 a.m.–9.00 a.m. (CET) and Sky wanted the hour 8.00 a.m.–9.00 a.m. back, *but* in its place, they would give us three hours from 5.00 a.m. to 8.00 a.m.

If we had not signed with them the week earlier, we would no doubt have received a phone call telling us that they needed

---

* See back of book for details.

the hour, but with no deal, in fact Goodbye Christian Channel Europe.

But because we had been obedient to God's voice, they were *locked* into our contract. They couldn't budge without our agreement. They *had* to consider the Christian Channel Europe.

After much prayer, we were convinced that although we would give up a premium hour, that three hours would give us the space to broadcast 'Kidz' TV', worship and Christian Music Television and allow us to present as a fully fledged channel. Much better than just two hours of solid preaching. And here comes God's miracle. In return for that premium hour, they gave us £175,000 *discount* on our airtime for the year! Only God Himself could have worked out such a remarkable discount for us for giving up the hour that had suddenly become invaluable to Sky.

We discovered that Transponder 47 was fast becoming a premium channel. Now, we were in the company of Sky Soap, Sky Sports 2, Sky Sports Gold, the History Channel and the Sci-Fi Channel. All these other channels were also only two to four hours a day, which made us the norm, rather than an outsider at an extended three hours. And that is how the Christian Channel has ended up broadcasting straight after the Sci-Fi Channel ends, between 5.00 a.m. and 8.00 a.m. Central European Time.

But we had reached the stage where every penny we possessed had been utilised and all resources were depleted. We had our ITC licence and a signed contract with BskyB, but we had come down to the end of our arm of the flesh and now . . . there was nothing left for us but God's miracle.

And so, on one sunny Friday morning in June, we arrived at the Heathrow Hilton where we were greeted by a young, enthusiastic young man, brimming over with energy. His name was Trevor Cockings.

Well, we opened our heart to Trevor, exchanged the vision

and left on our way to meet with Barbara and Gordon White
(a couple with a prophetic ministry) in Guildford.

They prophesied over us (which was taped), that God was
going to give us access to equipment and a building and that *in
but a few days* we would stand before two individuals who would
have great significance for the Christian Channel and ourselves.
(Note: this was Friday afternoon.)

Still a bit battered from our April trip to America, we
immediately placed the prophecy on the shelf.

Meanwhile, Rory was still believing for his air ticket back to
America to meet with some other ministries and to reconnect
with the men that we had met with on our previous disastrous
American trip.

Truly, we were almost at the end of ourselves. We had walked
by faith with God's dream in our hearts for so long believing
that *surely* those we shared with would realise that this was
indeed God's plan. God had worked His miracles and we now
had an ITC licence and a signed contract with Sky, but we were
at our human limit.

All our personal resources were exhausted, our grocery
cupboards were bare, we had a three-and-a-half-year-old little
girl and a six-month-old baby (who was waking from four to six
times a night). I was still suffering from violent nausea and
weakness (I was convinced that some satanist had found out
about the Christian Channel and was sticking pins into an effigy
of me!) and every avenue that could possibly fund the channel
was exhausted . . .

It was as though we were in the middle of a dark, black
tunnel from which there was no escape no matter how we tried.
After we'd been thrown into the pit, served time in Potiphar's
house, we were now languishing in prison, forgotten.

The weekend came and went. Every envelope was pounced
on avidly in case it was 'the' one, but five o'clock Monday afternoon (the deadline for Rory's air ticket) came and went with no
sign of a miraculous provision.

But you see, dearest reader, our faithful, wonderful heavenly Father is the God of all compassion and mercies. He is the God of the impossible, the God who turned water into wine, the God who raised Lazarus from the dead . . . and so, God was about to part our Red Sea in His ever miraculous way . . . and our miracle started with a phone call at five-fifteen on this gloomy summer's day.

A phone call that was about to change the destiny of the Christian Channel Europe.

Trevor's voice rang loud and clear through the receiver.

'Benny Hinn wants to see you in London . . . NOW!'

Above left: My mother—a young Jean, at the time she met Daddy.
Above right: My father—the very dashing and much *much* younger Hal 'Doc'
Koefman—the London doctor. Below left: Myself—a chubby four-year-old clutching
younger brother Robert (aged two) maybe a little too tightly!
Below right: The same—a few years later—time takes its toll!

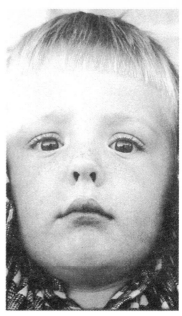

Above left: Lona (Rory's mother) and Bob Stephen (Rory's father)
on their wedding day. Above right: Rory aged three, in contemplative mood.
Below left: Rory—the up-and-coming musician. Below right: 1988
Alec-Gene days. (The high and mighty before they were greatly fallen!)

Above: Rory with Samantha, aged four. Below left: The cat licking the cream!—our very precious (and very strong!) Sammy, aged three. Below right: Our wonderful sunny little boy, Christian—aged twenty-two months.

Above: Us—no description needed!
Below: Rory—on the telephone to our lawyers . . . before we signed with BSkyB.
Behind the camera is our dear friend Howard Condor.

Above: Glory to God—the signed contract!

Above/Below: *Good Morning* crew in Wendy and Rory's living room.

Above: No, it's not Morticia Adams' Christmas Party—it's Wendy Alec's!
Below: Rory and Wendy looking at letters from viewers.

Above left: The more 'formalised' face of CCE—Richard Fleming! (our administrator). Above right: John Lilley editing *Good Morning Europe*. Below: Our *fantastic* team!

Above: Viewers from all across Europe queuing outside the Central Hall,
Westminster, for Dedication Service.
Below: In the spotlight on Dedication night.

Above: The wonderful, long-suffering Revd Colin Dye—perched precariously
on the chair at the Dedication to emphasise Rory's point!
Below: Introducing our effervescent, dynamic Jennifer Hughes—
presenter of Christian Music television across Europe.

Above: Pastor Ulf Ekman's special brand of Hallelujah fire.
Below: Rory sharing an informal moment with our
precious Pastor Benny at the Dedication.

Above: The actual moment of the Dedication
of The Christian Channel to the Lord Jesus Christ.

Chapter Ten

❖ ❖ ❖

The Parting of the Red Sea or Destiny on a Bus in London

*W*ell, there I was scrabbling for some semblance of make-up and the best remnants of our wardrobe, (which I'm sure Joseph didn't do when he was summoned before Pharaoh!).

Our baby-sitter was available, miraculously at a moment's notice, and so we hit the A4 into London, praying that we wouldn't be held up too long by five o'clock traffic.

We arrived in London, found a parking space and literally ran over the street to where Trevor's big gleaming bus was parked outside the hotel in Chelsea.

We were half an hour late. Yes, dear reader, we had kept Pastor Benny Hinn waiting in the bus for *half an hour*.

We climbed up the stairs of the bus, where we were greeted by Trevor, and turned to face the occupants.

Facing us was this arresting, elegantly dressed man who was

staring at us intensely. In fact, he looked at us quite sternly. (We *were* late.)

We were then introduced to Kent Mattox, David Delgardo and Pastor Benny's two elder daughters and the bus began its trip around London.

We started to share the vision of the Christian Channel Europe. Pastor Benny was, I must say, still staring at us with great scrutiny. I began to think twice about having chosen, in the flurry, my old faithful baggy black trousers.

Then, as we passed St Paul's Cathedral, Pastor Benny stopped the bus so that his daughters could see where they had filmed some of Mary Poppins. It was now pouring with rain.

Anyway, we all followed him out of the bus to look at St Paul's Cathedral and rather drizzled on, we re-entered the bus and continued to share about the Christian Channel.

By this time, I must add, the mascara I had used that day had reacted with my eye and was streaming all down one side of my face, and the rain had a disastrous effect on my hair!

So, there I was, feeling like a cross between the witch of Endor (from Shakespeare's *Macbeth*) and a London bag lady, facing these three men, with Rory answering Pastor Benny's enquiries as to the Channel's reach and were we *really* going to be able to launch—all completely valid questions that we had answered many times before.

But suddenly I remembered that day in January, after our initial contact with BSkyB, when out of the blue the Father had spoken to me as clear as a bell and said, '*Benny Hinn* will help you.'

Now, you must understand, that at that stage, this was completely *impossible*. The first and last time that we had ever seen or heard of Benny Hinn's ministry was in the mid 1980's at Rhema in South Africa when he ministered. We literally had no idea of the magnitude of this ministry and the effect that it was having worldwide. Benny Hinn to us was a man who we knew had had an incredible encounter with the Holy Spirit.

We were also in contact on a much more personal footing with many other international ministries and their media buyers who could and who, we were sure, *would* be the ones to assist the Christian Channel. We had tried to contact his office on a previous American trip—but to no avail.

But slowly and unmistakably, as Rory was reciting all the statistics back to Pastor Benny, the Father's voice came back as authoritatively as before: 'I told you, Benny Hinn *will help you.*'

And I found myself flashing back to our time in America and the frustration we had encountered.

Was everyone *only* interested in the commercial aspect of what they got out of it . . . did no one think *souls* any more? Had everyone who had had Christian television for years—had they all *forgotten* that they too had started by faith??

Was there *truly* someone who would see God's dream *before* it became a reality, who would see what God saw? Who would have the sensitivity and obedience to God to see beyond the two young people in front of them, beyond to a little David that could indeed overthrow the Goliath of the media in Europe? Did *everyone* want to control us?

And, finally, throwing all caution to the wind—it's easy to act as if you have no reputation when you quite patently *don't* have one! I am told that, with eyes flashing and (unfortunately) with my finger pointing (a bad trait!) straight at Pastor Benny, I blurted out 'Benny Hinn—have you forgotten how *you* started?'

There was a prolonged silence.

There I was, obviously staring at Pastor Benny in a rather fierce fashion with Kent, David and Trevor waiting with bated breath and Pastor Benny himself staring straight back at me.

And you know what, dear reader, suddenly the light of God broke through, and Pastor Benny's eyes started to twinkle with that simply marvellous Benny Hinn sense of humour.

Oh, dear friend, our mighty, powerful God is never confused.

Pastor Benny not only shook hands on a commitment to put *This is Your Day* on the Christian Channel twice a week, but he invited Rory over the next week to America to be a guest at his crusade in Louisville, Kentucky to introduce him to several people that he felt could assist us in the launch of the Christian Channel.

We left London that day knowing that Benny Hinn indeed sensed that God Himself was involved with the Christian Channel Europe and was prepared to assist in any way he could.

We also left with Kent Mattox's air miles, with two hundred pounds as a love offering from Trevor (bless you Kent and Trevor!) and with the face of God shining on his two young servants as we drove back to Surrey radiant with new hope and the assurance that God had indeed started to part the Red Sea.

And sure enough, Rory arrived a week later in Louisville, Kentucky to be at the crusade.

Now remember, that the last that we had experienced of Benny Hinn's services had been eight years before in South Africa. Rory's basic nature is to be an observer, but he said that the power of God was *so* strong during the crusade, reminiscent of his own Damascus Road experience in Ghana.

He described the wheelchairs that were lined up in rows. There was absolutely no doubt that the people were experiencing miraculous healings. Pastor Benny called him up to pray for him and the power of God was so intense that he was knocked off his feet.

I knew that for Rory to come home so affected by the power of God, something profound, something of great significance must be happening in Benny Hinn's ministry.

Well, Rory was looked after like royalty. Pastor Benny ensured that this young man from England had all his needs met. And then, God's counterplan came into play, one evening of the crusade when Rory turned to be introduced to the couple next to him.

'Hello—I'm Rory Alec, from England.'

'Hello—I'm Claud Bowers from Orlando, Florida.'

After the crusade, Claud flew Rory back to Orlando to his own television station, Superchannel 55, where he shared the vision with Claud and his wife, Freeda.

God's plan was brewing.

On the Sunday morning, Rory went to Pastor Benny's church, the World Outreach Centre, with Claud and Freeda.   And so it was that during the meeting, Pastor Benny looked over, pointing to Rory and Claud, saying, 'There's a divine connection between these two brothers.'

And indeed there was.

After the service, Rory asked for Pastor Benny to pray over a handkerchief as a contact point for my faith (as an antidote to any satanic pin-sticking!).

However, I must confess that after a few weeks, the anointed handkerchief went through the wash (and the tumble dryer) and I always had these vague doubts as to whether the anointing had been tumble dried out . . . (not quite the kind of question to ask at a partners' conference!). On top of that I seemed to have lost it in some obscure place, and became quite distressed for a few days, but I *am* healed!

Rory then flew back to London to rejoin us.

Almost immediately on his return, we received confirmation that Pastor Benny indeed *would* place his programme onto the channel twice a week and then, in the post, we received a gift of support from Benny Hinn Media Ministries—which was sent faithfully to us *every* month from the end of July right through to December.

God weaves His will and His divine connections to implement His divine purposes . . . and God in His infinite wisdom saw far beyond a little trip on a bus in London, through to a Christian television channel that would start to touch millions of lives across the continent of Europe. Interwoven in that plan was the crossing of Rory and Wendy Alec and Benny Hinn.

For you see, Europe—you are about to witness a revival unprecedented, such as you have never experienced before. A revival in which the Christian Channel Europe as a transport system is gaining momentum each day every week, thrusting light forward into where previously only darkness has reigned— and a great part of this is the transporting of ministries like Benny Hinn's that will stand out as a sign and a wonder in the midst of a stiff-necked and unbelieving generation, as a beacon of hope to the sick and the hopeless, showing forth God's love to a lost and dying Europe.

Truly, truly, I tell you, what we have thought to be the droplets of revival shall be as nothing in comparison to the mighty outpouring that is about to take place. And each ministry that is on the Christian Channel has been placed there by God Himself to turn the destiny of the churches across Europe and bring salvation to those whose hearts are filled with despair and hopelessness.

Let us never forget the honour that is due to men like Benny Hinn and all those who had the compassion and conviction to assist this ministry in its fledging early months when all that could be seen in the natural was just a dream.

For truly, God never forgets . . . and neither will we.

Chapter Eleven

❖ ❖ ❖

Money . . . Money . . . Money

*W*e were nearing the end of June and Rory was back in London, but we were still no closer to launching. We had no investors and therefore no capital. By now, Richard Fleming was spending his free time assisting us as our administrator and Paul Le Druillenac (who started his career as financial controller for Sky) had become CCE's financial director. All of this activity was coming out of our lounge with one computer, one fax machine, one telephone line, the kitchen being our board room.

Most of our ministry clients had agreed to come on the channel, the media buyers were all poised to sign the contracts and each day we were going forward towards the launch, but businesswise we were totally stunted because of the lack of funds.

Every Christian businessman that we had been introduced to in Europe seemed to be suffering from the recession and had just lost his business or was about to go bankrupt. Every businessman that they were networked to was also suffering.

Even the Full Gospel Businessman's Fellowship in Britain seemed to be having a wilderness experience. So many people were now enthused by the vision of the Christian Channel Europe, but nobody in Europe seemed to have a brass farthing to put together!!

We had been offered several deals, but each one of them involved the third party controlling the vision. This meant that they would be in control of all programming and would without doubt end up controlling the Christian Channel. This would be directly opposed to what the Lord had specifically instructed Rory—that no other ministry or television channel or group of businessmen could control the vision.

God had given us a direct mandate. First, the Christian Channel Europe was above all a *ministry,* before it was a business. Second, that God had a very defined programming schedule for Europe. His command to us was twofold—to broadcast the uncompromised Word of God and God's move of the Holy Spirit. God's promise to the fulfilment of this condition was that this channel would spearhead *revival* through Europe.

God had to be the Chairman of the board. We had to be free to put into operation everything that the Holy Spirit instructed us, or God's plan for the channel and its destiny in Europe would be watered down and could be aborted. This meant that only God's investor could fulfil all these conditions.

Now remember, Rory had met with Claud and Freeda Bowers in Florida. Claud had shown an interest in the Christian Channel, but we didn't know if it was a serious interest and if there would be strings attached that we could not accept. Claud was a shrewd businessman and we had now been around in Christian television long enough to realise that we needed to walk very circumspectly and with God's wisdom.

But the days passed and now our small team were working frantically to prepare everything for our launch date of

1 September. Still there was no capital. In fact, there was just *no money*, full stop.

Things had fast become more than desperate. Our telephone was cut because we could not pay the bill, Rory made his calls from the phone box with the Hampton Court traffic blaring out at sixty-five decibels. If the media buyers had known—they would have excommunicated us!

Two weeks into July, we got so much to the end of ourselves that Rory finally decided to leave a message on Claud's answering machine about the possibility of his charity's involvement with the Christian Channel Europe . . . just in case God had decided to use a man after all, and not just an angel to drop a wad of banknotes on the front doorstep! After most of the men we had met, we had more faith that God would use an angel and the wad of banknotes!

Well, Claud returned the call and booked his flight to come over to London, pointing out clearly that it was primarily to 'shop'.

On 21 July, we walked across Hampton Court Bridge from our house to the Mitre Hotel to meet with Claud Bowers. We sat across from him at the restaurant and poured our hearts out. He listened patiently and with great compassion as we unfolded the saga of the Christian Channel Europe in full technicolour. Oh!— God bless you, Claud!

The following morning, we met in the boardroom of the hotel with our administrator and financial director to present the channel's business proposal to Claud. We had come to the place where we knew beyond any shadow of a doubt that no man would be our source, but that God was *the only one* who could possibly give us the financial miracle desperately needed to launch the Christian Channel into its next phase.

To all and sundry, we were an unknown quantity. God would have to speak supernaturally to someone's heart. This could not just be a cold-blooded, analytical business decision. On top of the investment, our other condition was that the investor could have *no say or control* in the running of the Channel.

The presentation finished several hours later. Claud was moving that afternoon to the Metropole Hotel in London and would then fly back to Orlando, Florida. On his return to America, he would present the information to *his* charity's board as to whether they would be prepared to give the Christian Channel the investment needed.

As we walked out of the room, Claud pressed something into our hands.

It was a cheque for five thousand dollars.

God had seen our desperate and pressing needs, looked for a willing, obedient heart and had sent his servant all the way over from Florida to comfort us. This was but the beginning of our heavenly Father's goodness.

There we were left in London, standing (or rather—staggering) in faith, on tenterhooks, sweating profusely at intervals, waiting for Claud's decision from America.

Oh, all of you out there who are right now in a desperate financial situation, who are believing for a financial miracle for your family or your ministry—take heart. Your God is the same miracle-working God who was about to pour out a financial miracle into our lives.

Less than a week later, Claud rang with a decision from the board.

One hundred thousand dollars would be released as soon as the finer details could be worked out. Oh—how *good* God is when *His* purposes are involved. If He has to wake up a man or woman six thousand miles away to make sure that His project's needs are met—He *will* do it. He just looks for that obedient vessel who will listen and obey.

In fact, what was the greatest miracle of all was that, as we later found out, the board had actually made a decision to assist the Christian Channel *before* Claud flew out to London.

But *we* didn't know that!

Once the finer details with the board were ironed out, the money would be released into an escrow account here in London until we received the *three* approvals necessary before we could actually transmit our signal. But now we discovered that we needed a trust/charity to receive the funds from America. *Now* what? This application to become a charitable trust was a process that could take up to two years!

Once again, God was about to provide in the most miraculous way.

We received a telephone call that same week from our secular media lawyers, who at that stage didn't know our need for a charity. They advised us that another set of clients, who had contacted them months earlier, had set up a charity to launch daily Christian television into Europe and were about to close everything down due to the lack of support.

Richard Fleming, our administrator, contacted Mr Maurice Raybould and discovered that a team of Christian civil servants and lawyers had spent 1991 to 1993 forming not only a charity, but a charity relating to *Christian television*. In fact, the notes and conditions of the charity deed specified *everything* that the Christian Channel Europe embraced.

Not only was this a startling discovery, but the trustees of this charity went before the Lord in prayer and agreed with one accord to hand over the charity, lock, stock and barrel to the Christian Channel Europe.

God, in His infinite wisdom, had planned ahead and arranged for three experienced men with legal backgrounds to apply to the Charities Commission in 1991, with charitable status finally granted on 6 April 1993.

God had given us His *very own charity*, uniquely designed for the Christian Channel Europe, the charity that our viewers know today as the Angel Christian Television Trust.

Now it was time to negotiate for the second part of our launching capital!

Enter Dr Morris Cerullo.

Via many long and varied faxes from San Diego, we had at last reached the agreement that for a substantial yearly discount, Dr Cerullo would forward his entire year's sponsorship to the Christian Channel upfront.

After many many phone calls, faxes, more faxes and more phone calls, and several personal meetings with Lynne Hodge, Dr Cerullo's assistant, everything was agreed and we received a second portion of our launching capital.

Dr Cerullo is a shrewd businessman and extremely smart, and it is a tremendous credit to him that he was prepared to advance us the yearly payment with no guarantees that we would actually survive more than the first month. He has always displayed a genuine affection for Rory and me, and monitored our progress with great interest after that first meeting at Grosvenor House. On one occasion he telephoned us from San Diego, confounded as he had just heard 'little David' was actually in negotiation with BSkyB!

Rory and I appreciated that his willingness to upfront the year's fee was his contribution to the launching of God's miracle channel. It was Dr Cerullo's way of saying, 'I believe God is with you. I'll support you.' And so, this too went into our escrow account.

Now there was only one problem—*no* money could be released from the escrow account until we had the three approvals that Sky needed to be authorised before we could finally broadcast.

On 15 August, we had re-signed the contract with BSkyB for the new three-hour block from 5.00 a.m. to 8.00 a.m. Immediately on signing, Sky (as the lead partner) applied for approval for the Christian Channel from BT (British Telecom), Astra and the Government of Luxembourg.

And there it simmered.

The middle of August found us with still no premises for the Christian Channel.

Europe's potential first daily Christian television channel was at present operating from a three-bedroom, three-storey character house in Surrey, a stone's throw from the River Thames, situated immediately behind Hampton Court village.

Our lounge had become the working area. In fact the whole house had turned into a working area! We had at that stage one fax machine, one telephone line and had been working avidly at expanding into Hampton Court village or thereabouts, into a two or three-room office.

However, *every* place we saw that we felt could be utilised, turned out, on application for further details, to have just been let—*every* time. We were becoming perplexed. All we wanted was a small office in the local area, and yet every single premises that looked even vaguely suitable was immediately snatched, seemingly from under our very noses, and now we had just six weeks till our launch.

God was about to provide for the Christian Channel again, in the most remarkable way.

A few weeks earlier, I had felt led to phone the Family Channel to ask their marketing department to recommend a good marketing company in the cable and satellite industry. They had recommended a young company who were actually based at the Family Channel and who had the Family Channel as one of their accounts.

One sweltering mid-August morning, we arrived at the Family Channel in Maidstone, Kent, had our meeting with the marketing company, and were on our way out, when we were introduced to the marketing director who offered to take us on a five-minute tour of the Family Channel Studios.

Well, what *we* didn't know, but what God surely knew, was that this five-minute tour was to turn into over an hour and a half, and that the Family Channel were planning to rent out some of their studio site to independent cable and satellite channels . . .

We left that afternoon with a deal on the table for discussion.

By the first week of September, we were resident in the Family Channel Studios in Maidstone. God had given us the perfect address to launch from—Television Centre, Vinters Park, Maidstone.

We were given a section of the first floor as our production offices, an edit suite that was totally locked out to the Christian Channel, sixteen dedicated telephone lines, desks, chairs, a betacam recording machine and access to three studios as and when they were required.

On top of this, we had a rentfree period for *all* of the above until January 1996 (which we desperately needed). How wonderful is our God's provision. *God* knew we were truly seeking first His kingdom, and He added on to us His tremendous provision for the channel's premises during this crucial launch period. We didn't even *ask* Him for it. This was far and above all we could ask or think!

Remember, the earlier prophecy that had said in a few days we would stand before two men, had also stated that God was bringing us the right buildings and equipment (edit suite) . . .

As a matter of interest, the final element to that prophecy was that there would be yet a third man, in a few months' time, of great importance, who would be *right* on time . . . So, we don't know who or how or where, but we are completely assured that this third man is about to arrive on the Christian Channel's doorstep by fax, phone, bus(!) . . . and that he won't be late . . . for surely God has proven Himself faithful to us time after time.

What an exciting time we live in . . . what exciting days!

Chapter Twelve

❖   ❖   ❖

Final Frontier

*W*ell, now the application by Sky on the Christian Channel's behalf for the approvals from BT, Astra and the Government of Luxembourg was underway.

We gained the approval from BT fairly easily; Astra was a more lengthy process but was agreed by early September but now the Government of Luxembourg started to drag its heels.

Sky had informed us that these approvals were nothing more than a formality. They reassured us that they would take approximately ten days. The application to the Government of Luxembourg had been submitted about eighteen days previously, and still there was no sign of an answer.

The money that was in the escrow account could not be released until we had all three approvals. So, although we had over a hundred thousand pounds launch capital in the escrow account, we quite categorically couldn't touch a penny of it.

It was early September. We had less than twenty days to launch and quite patently, although God had released His funds to us, they were now stuck. We couldn't pay for our design, our marketing or our PR company. We couldn't *even* pay for one run of our launch brochures.

To make it worse—if the Government of Luxembourg for some obscure and satanic reason decided *not* to grant the Christian Channel Europe approval, *everything* would be lost. There would be *no* Christian Channel Europe. *Everything* was now hinging on the Government of Luxembourg.

Now we had another crisis of decision. Should we call all our activities to a halt?

We had already commissioned all our onscreen graphics, our launch brochures, started to edit the first month's programmes and received most of our material from Europe and America.

Should we delay our launch *yet* again a month to November? And finally, if we didn't, would we *dare* to go ahead with our press launch on 27 September?

Suddenly visions loomed of Rory and me standing in front of the London press telling them we didn't actually exist. After all the struggles, all the crises we had been through, we seemed to be up against a rockface.

Remember the grand sceptics, eyes were all fixed on the little upstart David, waiting to see if maybe he *could* just possibly, by some outside chance, be the one to kill Goliath. They had already scoffed at our previous postponement—another one would cause complete disbelief in the camp of observers.

We also sensed that if we put our launch off *again*, all the media buyers would get cold feet and probably decide that we would never launch and possibly withdraw their support. So finally we said, 'Father—do you *want* us to postpone till November or to go ahead and launch by faith?'

And God said, 'LAUNCH.'

And then we said, 'Father—do you want us to announce the press conference in London on 27 September?'

And God said, 'ANNOUNCE.'

We took the longest deep breath we had ever taken, knowing that if we had *not* heard God's voice on this issue, our bones would be fit for the vultures in the field.

And so, we worked day by day towards the launch by faith, with no budget, knowing that in the natural, the house could come crashing down around us like a pack of cards.

We started the countdown to the press conference. The twenty-sixth was the final day to cancel. We could not legally go ahead and announce to the country that we were launching unless Sky had the final approval from Luxembourg.

Fifteen days to launch . . . no word from Luxembourg.

Ten days to launch . . . no word from Luxembourg.

Then, miracle of miracles, five thousand pounds arrived all the way from Pastor Ulf Ekman's church—Word of Life in Uppsala, Sweden! *(Rory had met a few months earlier with Bo Sanders, Pastor Ulf Ekman's head of television, and had been invited to Word of Life where he received a wonderful, enthusiastic welcome from both Pastor Ulf and the Swedish people. Rory loves Sweden! Since then, Pastor Ulf has shown an ongoing and zealous commitment to seeing the gospel preached through the Christian Channel in Europe and has been a true encouragement and example of faith to both Rory and me.)*

Five days to launch . . . no approvals.

Then it dawned on us—that Luxembourg own the entire strip of airspace called Astra in Europe. This was surely where the Prince of the Power of the air had his stronghold in Europe. *Now* we started to realise this was Satan's final bulwark.

It was at this crucial stage that the secular PR company we were working with got extremely nervous. They were arranging our national press conference—would they get paid?

Three days to launch—no approvals. Launch budget still tied up in escrow.

Now *we* got extremely nervous—'Hello, God . . . Hi! It's

Wendy . . . it's Rory . . . your children . . . cough . . . ahem . . . we seem to have a slight hiccup here . . . earth to heaven . . . S.O.S!'

The twenty-fifth of September arrived. One day to the press conference . . . no approvals.

The twenty-sixth of September . . . we were with Howard Condor (an old friend) in his graphics studio, cutting the final stage of our audio-visual press presentation together . . . no approvals.

Then, late that afternoon, after *every* boundary of faith had been pushed to the limit . . . a fax came through on the studio's fax machine—THE GOVERNMENT OF LUXEMBOURG APPROVES . . .

Glory to God in the highest—the greatest victory in the heavenlies over Luxembourg had been won. Our mighty, powerful God had come through in such splendour. If ever the powers of darkness had wanted to roadblock the move of God, it was *now*. And you know what, dear reader, they couldn't. This was God's television channel. This was *not* just a good idea. This was *God's* idea and He was jealous over it. *Nothing* would stop His baby from being born.

And so it was that on Wednesday 27 September 1995, ourselves and Pastor Colin Dye gathered together in front of the national press in London.

God's baby was about to be born—unscathed, perfectly formed, the parents a bit the worse for wear from the labour, but nothing that a cup of tea and a biscuit couldn't fix!

Chapter Thirteen

❖ ❖ ❖

Facing the Press

*I*t was Wednesday morning, 27 September. There, seated facing the press in the Cumberland Hotel, Mayfair were myself, Rory and Pastor Colin Dye—the innocents about to be thrown to the wolves!

We had approached Colin months before when we quite patently had nothing. He had listened patiently and very politely to our dreams of a Christian television channel but we must admit that we had left slightly disheartened, not knowing if we had managed to impart the vision effectively.

However, just over a fortnight later, we received the most heartwarming, marvellous letter from Pastor Colin, saying that he had prayed about our request for him to be on our council of reference and that God had spoken to him. He had a great conviction that God was with us, would consider it a privilege to be a part of what God was clearly involved in and would assist us in any way possible.

Through the rocky times during our initial launch period Colin has been a consistent source of great wisdom and encouragement and has become a trusted friend. (We do so enjoy his company!) We honour him for the commitment that he has shown not only to the Christian Channel Europe, but to Rory and myself personally.

Anyway, so there were the three of us facing the pack of wolves: European Broadcast News, the *Guardian*, *The Times*— to name but a few.

One particular photographer in the front row was staring at us as if we had come off Noah's ark itself. In fact, he kept staring throughout our whole presentation in a rather disconcerting manner as though we were from another planet.

I think that the journalists were prepared for some sort of cross between Songs of Praise, Jimmy Swaggart and the local choral evensong. Instead the showreel started with DC Talk and contemporary Christian music. *That* blew a few of the religious cobwebs away!

Then there was the unmistakable lady in red—religious correspondent for a particular newspaper —who was to become a long-term challenger of the Christian Channel.

After the initial press interviews had been conducted, it was time for the photographs. There was an attempt to get Rory and me to stand on chairs against a backdrop of a little girl with JESUS written on a bandana around her forehead and Rory refused, visualising headlines 'Christian Channel brainwashes your children'. When we saw the scathing output of certain journalists (especially the one in red) we were relieved that he had taken that stand. God bless the secular press.

Then it was time for BBC Radio Five Live which Rory and Colin conducted, also VIVA Radio and then onto the regional radio stations—BBC Radio Northampton, BBC Lincs, BBC Derby, BBC Scotland, BBC Suffolk, BBC Kent, BBC

Newcastle, BBC Wilts, BBC Southern Counties, BBC Lancaster and BBC York.

That night, news of the impending launch of the Christian Channel was broadcast across Europe on EBN (European Business News) and RAI (Italian State Television), and also on Austrian television.

Now we had three days to go until our first broadcast. All systems go!

Rory and I were buried in the edit suite from morning till midnight, overseeing the cutting together of the programmes, putting together the final television formats, and directing the channel's operations frantically from the 'black hole'!

Then came a phone call from Peter Stremes, former programming director for United Artists cable (Telewest/SBC), whom we had tried to persuade a year earlier to take the channel. He had seen us on European Broadcast News the previous evening. He would send us a contract.

God was amazing! This was the biggest cable operator in the United Kingdom and they had approached *us* before we even launched.

The phone continued to be jammed with enquirers, critics, enthusiasts and an incessant stream of requests for radio and television interviews.

Our staff was growing day by day at a rapid rate. This was because we took brief respite from our 'black hole' at intervals to interview all kinds of sometimes 'strange' Steven Spielberg enthusiasts among others . . . Some of these stayed!! I will be kind and not incriminate them except to say that it was the first and only time that I ever saw our scheduler in a black suit and tie (he looked remarkably like a funeral director!).

In fact we were getting quite crammed by now, working frantically for our launch on Sunday the first of October.

Friday 29 September dawned—this was Rory's thirtieth birthday. The edit suite was visited with a Pingu birthday cake (the only one available from the nearest Sainsbury's store), and he dutifully endured 'Happy Birthday' sung by the now rather motley but very enthusiastic, if not slightly off-key, Christian Channel crew!

Saturday came and went and we were still frantically editing. The tapes *just* got couriered to Sky in time for the deadline.

And so, at five o'clock in the morning on Sunday the first of October, as soon as the Sci Fi Channel signed off, the Christian Channel logo appeared for the first time on Transponder 47 across nineteen nations in Europe.

The Sunday papers were bought in a great flurry that day . . . especially the *Independent on Sunday* (several of our fervent supporters, including my mother, raided about ten copies from the local corner shop!) which had run a three-page colour spread in their colour magazine section that morning.

I have to say that although Peter Popham's article was at times scathing, it was *certainly* entertaining reading! After citing Benny Hinn, Kenneth and Gloria Copeland, to name but a few, Popham wrote: '*Such stuff is not going to help an Anglican rector's cornflakes go down, but there is little doubt that it will find an audience.*' He certainly did his homework—except for one glaring error where he cited Gerald Coates as our pastor in Esher. Untrue. We had lived in Esher, though. Popham continued:

American television audiences have been subjected to such hysterical blandishments for years. But in Britain, religious television still means the sober proprieties of Songs of Praise.

The established churches are still bitterly opposed to the opening up of Britain to an influx of televangelism, and so, as a pre-emptive strike against it, had planned to launch in the spring of next year a cable channel, Ark 2.

Backed by the Church of England, the Catholics, the Methodists and other denominations, it will present the safe, responsible, balanced face of mainstream British Christianity.

Now their plans have been spoiled. Two young, charismatic Christians have come out of nowhere and accomplished the thing the churches dreaded the most. They have enabled the televangelists to get a foot inside British television's door.

Their names are Rory and Wendy Alec, born-again Christians who arrived in the UK from South Africa four years ago. Their baby is Christian Channel Europe (CCE) and it arrives on British screens by courtesy of Astra, the television satellite company.

He continued (at least he called us charming . . . to make up for the other two and a half pages of descriptions that weren't quite so flattering!):

The Alecs are charming, but even before transmission began, they had incurred the wrath of the religious establishment. The sweetly reasonable Ernest Rea, head of religious broadcasting at the BBC, said, 'It's a very unwelcome development. British evangelists'—presumably those within the mainstream—'have very clearly decided not to repeat the US televangelist experience—not to exploit the vulnerability of viewers—not to proselytise overtly.'

Well, and on it went. Popham did mention however that *'Starting from small independent churches, South Africa's religious revival has grown so fast and so far that it has touched every denomination in the country.'* And then, as though we were about to beam up a strange brand of Afrikaaner neonazi propaganda over Britain, and were part of the SS Jugend, he stated, *'Young, gifted and fanatical, the Alecs are its perfect exemplars.'*

During the next few days of our launch period, interviews were conducted with Talk Radio UK, BBC Radio 4 Sunday, ITV Meridian and BBC Radio World Service.

We then had a call inviting Rory onto *Newsnight* with Jon Snow. This was cancelled just an hour before, due an overriding story which broke from Gibraltar.

Articles appeared in the *Guardian*, the *Evening Standard*, the *Observer*, the *Daily Mail*, throughout the regional print media and the media trade press. The headlines that week included *'All rise for dawn chorus'*, *'TV blessings from on high'*, *'Do not convert your dish'*, *'Heavens above!'*, *'Tele-evangelism comes to Britain'* and *'Breakfast with God!'*

One London publication even warned the 'purveyors of erotica' to *'watch out as CCE's statement of faith promises eternal damnation for the unrepentant sinner!'*

Then we were approached by BBC 1 and invited onto *Good Morning with Anne and Nick* scheduled for early November. During this time, we were also approached by the senior editor of BBC1's *Everyman* documentary programme who were interested in producing a fifty-minute documentary on the Christian Channel Europe.

I quote from the BBC's letter to us:

It is our job to inform the public of important developments to the religious scene and it is now our belief that your venture is such a development and could well change the religious landscape of Europe of the future.

During this time period, we were still spending eighteen-hour days in the edit suite overseeing the channel's output. Meanwhile, back in administration, the main focus became setting up the computers to handle the response that had started to flood into the channel.

In between this, Rory and Richard started to visit churches in Scotland, Ireland, Germany and Sweden. The body of Christ were fast becoming aware of the Christian Channel's existence and were excited!

Unhappy subscribers to cable were starting to demand the Christian Channel and suddenly we were receiving calls from cable operators nationwide asking for proposals and contracts.

Christian Music Television was starting to take off and was becoming a huge hit with the young people around Europe.

It was now late October and we had to give the BBC an answer as to whether or not we would go ahead with the *Everyman* documentary.

We had been given a quick indoctrination into the baptism of press fire, so we prayed very seriously about our involvement in *Everyman*, but we felt that God said, 'Yes'. We met with the producer Chris Mann and agreed to a shooting schedule in early November. Part of this agreement involved allowing Chris Mann's crew to film us during our trip to Birmingham to appear on the *Anne and Nick* show. So there we were in Birmingham, not only about to appear on the *Anne and Nick* show (which was intimidating enough), but we had the BBC 1 *Everyman* crew following every movement.

(Yes—you all want to know, 'What were Anne and Nick like?' They were great.)

We actually had an excellent conversation about Christian values and Anne Diamond's concern about the adverts for the Playboy Channel now being flighted on Sky, *before* we went live. Unfortunately, as the Christian Channel promo was rolled in, I saw Anne catch sight of Jeff Fenholt preaching in his inimitable style and saw her eyes start to bulge in a rather, 'This is Bible-bashing fundamentalism . . . *what* have we got here?' expression.

So, from the warm, expansive attitude she had previously shown, she did become slightly more on guard, but Nick continued, undeterred. All went smoothly except, as the

Everyman documentary revealed (God bless you, Chris Mann) my false fingernail flew off in Nick's face just as we closed!

But the most amazing outcome of the *Anne and Nick* show was the actual telephone response of the viewers. On the show, the producers allowed just two responses out—one for Christian television and one against. Behind the scenes they had, in that short space of time, 104 telephone calls from the public. 100 *for* Christian television in Britain and only *four* against. How I wish the world had known *that* fact! God's people are excited!

November continued in a flurry of activity, visiting churches, preparing marketing proposals, sourcing new programmes, expanding our cable penetration, sending out mailshots. Eventually, we distributed more than one hundred and eighty thousand Christian Channel brochures across Britain and mainland Europe.

Meanwhile, the BBC 1 crew were still avidly filming our progress. They filmed us moving into the house in Maidstone, Rory and Richard visiting Ulf Ekman's church in Uppsala, Sweden, where CCE has always received a fantastic welcome; they even filmed us stirring soup over the stove. In fact, our lives became theirs for most of November.

The airing date for the documentary called *The Miracle Channel* was scheduled for 28 January 1996 and the flack began.

The *Morning Star* labelled us as '*fundamentalist, Bible-bashing*' and '*a disturbing phenomenon*' (*Morning Star,* London, 27 Jan), while the *Observer* proclaimed that the channel '*preaches hell fire to sinners, material prosperity for believers, and targets vulnerable young viewers*' (the *Observer,* London, 28 Jan).

The *Sunday Times* stated:

> *Strangely for* Everyman, *no questions are asked, no debate raised. It is in fact a free puff for Rory and Wendy*

who are filmed as 'blessed' parents at home, and as
'blessed' presenters at work on a channel where people
claim to be 'genuinely excited by what God is doing', as if
he were the new Tarantino.

The *Financial Times* declared, *'Everyman' on BBC reveals*
what a flap the CCE channel has caused in the dovecoat of
religious broadcasting.'
The *Newcastle Evening Chronicle* warned:

Keep your head down, lock the doors and pull out the TC
plug—the telly evangelists are at the door. And judging
by last Sunday's Everyman *on BBC1 we need all the*
protection we can gather. Fifty minutes of what was in
effect an unchallenged promotion of Christian Channel
Europe was frightening.

And of course, *The Times* did mention that Rory and I were
'brain dead', God bless them.

Well, we were able to watch a preview of the documentary
three days before it went out across Great Britain.

We had been filmed answering our critics' comments in the
final *Everyman* interview by the producer Chris Mann, who
afterwards aired a genuine relief that we seemed only mildly
shaken by the overt criticism. (We had actually been prepared
for far, *far* worse!)

I have to confess that when we actually viewed our two most
scathing critics on camera, Ernest Rea (Head of Religious
Programming, BBC) and A. Gill, TV Critic for the *Sunday Times*,
I found both, although at times apoplectic in their
condemnation of the channel and on occasion remarkably
scathing, to be sincere men.

And in Ernest Rea's defence, he had, after the actual broadcast of the documentary, called us 'genuinely sincere',
although he did add that we were in a 'spiritual cocoon'.

The *Everyman* documentary was aired on Sunday 28 January and the reaction was incredible! The Christian Channel phones rang off the hook!

There was also an interesting and heated response to the BBC. Here are some of the comments quoted from their Factual Unit report:

'A marvellous programme.'

'Complained the programme came across as mere propaganda for the couple featured.'

'Thanks the BBC for showing the power of God!'

'Felt the programme gave too much publicity to CCE.'

'Felt it was a very good, impartial, fair and very interesting programme.'

'It was a very lopsided and anti-view on the CCE.'

'Absolutely excellent. I support everything the programme was depicting.'

'Said the BBC ought to take a leaf out of the Christian Channel's book.'

(I'm sure that that probably turned the longsuffering Mr Rea a shade of puce!)

One comment that I really enjoyed was a pastor who phoned the BBC to say that *'John Wesley was "laughed at" when he first founded the Methodist Church, so the critics of the Christian Channel are used to it!'*

Then the Christian Channel was featured on the BBC programme *Right to Reply* where again the increasingly tormented Mr Rea was taken to task by one of the BBC's born-again viewers on the attitude he displayed to the Christian Channel on the documentary.

All in all, we were pleasantly surprised by the treatment that the BBC gave the channel.

You see, we have *never ever* taken the press seriously. And we never will. The only press we take seriously is the press release from our heavenly Father. It is what He says that counts. Yes—

of course they call us heretics, Bible bashers, fundamentalists. They called Jesus a lunatic! The religious spirits across Europe are *howling* with rage.

Somehow, someway, two thousand years ago the devil, looking for a King who would be born to power, riches and influence, let the son of God, born in a humble stable, slip through his hands, and so it was the same with the Christian Channel Europe; the devil had let the infant channel slip through his hands and he was *enraged.*

He had been looking for those with money and power and earthly sway, for those are *his* yardstick. You see, dear reader, the one thing that literally *confounds* the devil is the anointing.

For God chooses whom He will choose and whereas Satan's basis for choosing is natural strength and ability, God's list of 'who's who' is based on those He has foreordained to serve Him from the beginning of time. It is also based on a willing and available heart, on His calling and His anointing.

God chose Moses the stutterer, David the shepherd boy and even His own Son was born of a humble carpenter. And His criteria have never changed. For what God holds more precious than gold is our total surrender—for surely, friends, He looks at our hearts.

Chapter Fourteen

❖ ❖ ❖

The Eurothon

*W*e were now faced with an *interesting* situation.

From the first of October, we had thirty-four thousand pounds' worth of revenue coming in every month, but our overheads (at the bare minimum) added up to approximately eighty-seven thousand pounds a month, leaving us with a monthly deficit of over forty-seven thousand pounds.

God had told us to launch by faith and we were being obedient. But we had some distinct disadvantages that were continually threatening our survival.

Firstly, we were a brand new ministry and therefore had no partner base, launching into Christian television which was completely uncharted territory in Europe.

Where churches already *had* their own equipment, or were starting to fund it, *we* as the first daily Christian television channel in Western Europe had to *hire* our equipment every shoot at exorbitant prices.

In America, the television station's financial needs are met by holding *telethons*, which is where the running costs of television are put before the viewers and an ongoing appeal is made for up to a week to support the work of God through Christian television.

Now, in Europe there were two obstacles.

First, we were under *no* circumstances and on *no* condition allowed to appeal for funds on air, under the ITC regulations.

Second, because of some of the excesses and misuses in America, fund-raising had become such a contentious issue in Europe—one we wanted to steer well clear of.

But *what* were we to do? *How* would we survive? Media ministries were plummeting all around us at an alarming rate, through lack of funds. They were *all* struggling and seemed to be issuing unending pleas for finance.

Why God always seemed to call us to the impossible only He knows! You see, every step that we have taken, only God has been able to bring us through.

We were not starting small, as all the big Christian televisions had started off in America and grown. For example, CBN started with one small station in Charlotte; TBN started with one station in Los Angeles.

Here we were, starting off by God's grace with access to the *whole* of Western Europe—nineteen nations—on the most exclusive European satellite, with airtime immediately taking us into the big league costing thousands of pounds, combined with television overheads which aren't Mickey Mouse.

Channel 5's launch budget was reported to have been two hundred million pounds. Ours was one hundred and sixteen thousand pounds. And it was gobbled up almost on our first day.

As the Christian Channel, we had in an incredibly short space of time grown an amazing family of thousands right across Europe—growing at a rapid rate every single day—but the last thing we wanted to do to all of our new excited viewers was to ask for money! Rory and I were adamant: we didn't want our new Christian Channel family of viewers to feel pressurised to give.

But things were becoming desperate. How would we survive through Christmas?

Then we received a phone call. Claud and Freeda Bowers were coming to London—to visit Harrods and to shop. Now this time, we could hear in Claud's voice, he really meant *shop*!

Two weeks before Christmas, Claud, his wife Freeda and the Superchannel 55 team arrived in London. First stop, the Christian Channel. After dinner together, Rory approached Claud about holding the Eurothon.

Let me explain. When we had been in America the previous year on our disastrous trip, Rory and I had stared wide-eyed at four in the morning, watching Paul Crouch, of America's largest Christian television network, ask his viewers to support the work of Christian television financially.

We had stared at each other, open-mouthed.

What if *we* could hold a telethon, not in Europe, but in America, where people understood the tremendous power of Christian television and the influence that it could carry. Where the people had a heart for missions and would see the urgency of getting the gospel out to the dark continent . . . Europe. We wouldn't call it a telethon . . . we would call it a *Eurothon*.

Claud and Rory met for breakfast the next morning. Once again, God had lured Claud out to Britain to 'shop' and dumped on him!

God bless you, Claud, for your obedience to the prompting of the Lord. We honour you for your unhesitating willingness to hear God when He spoke to you.

Claud, unbeknown to us, was conducting his own television

channel's telethon for a week starting on 3 January. He had already planned a night on the following Monday where he would raise funds for Europe and Haiti.

It could easily dovetail. On his return to America, Claud would approach the other independent Christian television station owners and see if they would each be prepared to link up through America for one night to raise funds from their viewers for the Christian Channel.

'Oh!' we said brightly, 'what about Benny Hinn being our special guest?

Claud stared at us slightly sceptically!

And so, over Christmas, we waited, totally at peace that this was God's channel, not knowing if the Eurothon would happen; then towards the end of December, we received a call from Claud—the Eurothon was on.

Now, if you cast your mind back to our first disastrous trip to America, you will remember that in prophecy God had said that we would find great favour with the men we would meet and we had deduced that great favour equalled money.

Well, Claud had returned and approached every one of the men that we had met on our previous seemingly futile trip to America who owned a major independent Christian television station and asked these same men if they would get involved in the Eurothon, and, wait for God's favour. Saints—*every single man had agreed to co-host the Christian Channel Eurothon.* That first trip had come to fruition in *God's time*, not *our* time— nearly nine months later.

Oh, how disillusioned and disappointed we get when God's plan seems to come to nought, only to find that He, in His magnificent overview has it all *meticulously* planned far better than we can ever dream, hope or imagine! What a miracle-working God we serve!

Jerry Rose of WCFC Chicago, Marcus Lamb of KMTX TV 29, Dallas, Garth Kuns of WTCT Channel 27,

Illinois and Russ Bixler of Cornerstone TV 40, Pittsburgh, had *all* agreed to devote at least three hours of their prime Saturday night airtime to the Christian Channel Europe. Claud Bowers in Orlando, would host the Eurothon and . . . wait for it, friends . . . Pastor Benny Hinn had agreed to take time out from his hectic schedule to be our special guest that evening.

Oh—the goodness of God towards us—what delight He has in watching His children believe for the impossible.

And you know, God actually had to slap our wrists the week before we left and say, 'Get in faith for the money, kids!' Because we had almost overlearnt our lesson and were saying, 'Whatever God wants—it's up to Him.'

So now we felt we had *His permission* to believe, we roused ourselves, and started to believe for two hundred thousand pounds to be raised in America.

And so, on 6 January, we boarded the Virgin flight to Orlando and were about to enter one of the most exciting weeks of our life.

(The greatest miracle is that as I actually write this, our monthly deficit has been brought down *supernaturally* fast by both the faithfulness of our partners and business wisdom, to a miraculous breakeven! God has already brought in a consistent extra flow of resources to cover forty-seven thousand pounds of deficit a month since we started. Most television channels run at a loss for years.)

Chapter Fifteen

❖ ❖ ❖

This Was Our Day!

*A*s the Virgin airliner drew nearer to Florida, there was a definite change in the spiritual climate and we felt a great anticipation. We were not to be disappointed.

We were picked up, taken to the hotel where we were to rest and told we'd be collected the following morning to attend the ten o'clock service at the World Outreach Centre, Pastor Benny Hinn's church.

Well, it was as though we walked into a tidal wave of blessing. Oh, how wonderful it was to bask in the anointing of God. All through the Sunday and Monday, there was a very real presence of Almighty God surrounding us. We laid our heads down on the pillow in blessing. We woke up to more blessing. Next, we were taken shopping!

Janice, a member of the World Outreach Centre, had been led by the Lord to buy Rory a whole new wardrobe and Claud's wife, Freeda, was buying me one too! What generous-hearted people.

This was *incredible*! Suddenly everywhere we looked was abundance and blessing.

You have to understand that for over four years we had been living in a place called 'Paying the Price' and there had been no luxuries. I had literally worn one pair of favoured comfortable boots through two winters; my favourite trousers were on their last legs; my make-up was almost finished; my perfume bottles were empty; and I had one pair of earrings. Rory was in the same situation because the only thing that mattered was to launch Christian television into Europe, not to look like an advert for Chanel!

But it seemed as if God was literally determined to bless us. I cannot tell you what it was like to suddenly have a beautiful watch and lovely earrings, to have my favourite 'Estee' perfume and some gorgeous clothes! And there was Rory with new apparel, looking like a young up-and-coming preacher.

God was blessing us to fulfil His purpose. He was about to launch us into a phase of ministry where we would be sharing from platforms all across Europe and America, where we would be speaking at churches and conventions, be interviewed by the press and generally be in both the public and secular eye. So we needed to look the part.

We woke up, again surrounded by the presence of God—this was our day—the Christian Channel Eurothon! Late that afternoon, we were still editing together the inserts for that evening. Frantically we changed into our Eurothon attire, our make-up was applied . . . and the opening credits started to roll.

Claud Bowers introduced Marcus Lamb and Russ and Norma Bixler who had flown in from Dallas and Pittsburgh respectively for the evening's events.

Colin Dye, Wynne Lewis, Reinhard Bonnke, Jesse Duplantis and Dr Morris Cerullo had all pre-taped enthusiastic and supportive messages encouraging America to support the Christian Channel both in prayer and financially.

Our clips of British and European News were aired and then we were introduced.

And the telephones started to ring.

And they rang . . . and they rang . . . in fact, for at least an hour, there wasn't a single telephone that wasn't ringing. America was excited.

Then at eight-thirty, special guest Pastor Benny Hinn arrived.

And the phones rang . . . and they rang . . . and they rang . . . pledging a thousand dollars . . . seventy dollars . . . a thousand dollars . . . sixty . . . fifty . . . a thousand . . . and on and on . . .

Pastor Benny had to leave by ten o'clock, but he very kindly promised the viewers that he would pray over all the pledges the next morning in church.

By the end of the evening over two hundred and fifty thousand dollars had been pledged to the development of the Christian Channel Europe.

We serve an amazing God.

We fell into bed exhausted but exhilarated—I'm sure we slept with beaming smiles on our faces that night (of relief). God in His great compassion had opened a way where it seemed there was no way and made His face to shine upon us.

We arrived at the World Outreach Centre the following morning where Pastor Benny prayed with Claud Bowers and ourselves over the pledges of the people.

Pastor Benny shared that he wanted to tape a week's programmes of *This is Your Day* with our address on the end of each programme, enabling the American viewers to send in offerings if they felt able to do so to assist the work in Europe.

'We will work together for a whole week and ask people all over the world to help this new beginning . . . and I believe that God will give you a million dollars,' he said.

How exciting, we said.

'How interesting,' the British media said.   And therein lies a tale (which we shall return to later in the chapter).

But now, it was time to head up Texas way.

We arrived in Dallas for a whirlwind one-night visit, where we got reacquainted with Joni and Marcus Lamb and spent the evening with them on their show. We were also privileged to meet that wonderful gentleman, Harald Bredesen, and were able to sit with him on the sofa, listening to the most simple but effective teaching on how to receive the Holy Spirit that I think I have ever heard.

Then onto Tulsa, where we booked into the hotel, situated directly opposite the Oral Roberts University. The following day we were due to meet with Richard Roberts. So, early the next morning, we were picked up and escorted all the way up to the seventh floor where we were taken into Richard Roberts' executive office.

It became evident early on in the conversation that Richard had a tremendous pastoral heart for the students at Oral Roberts University, and a tremendous desire to see the fulfilment of all God's promises for the university. We left with the understanding that our paths would cross again in Europe later that year, which indeed they did at the '96 Eurospirit Conference in Holland.

We conducted some radio interviews and then it was over to Victory Christian Centre to meet with that gentlemen of pastors, Pastor Billy Jo Daugherty.

Oh, what a gentle-hearted, wise man he is and what a heartfelt welcome he gave to us. It was so evident that Pastor Billy Jo had a fire lit by the Holy Spirit in his heart for the continent of Europe.

We shared the vision with him and he listened intently. Then, looking at us with great earnestness, he said: 'Nations are in the balance.' As he spoke, the Holy Spirit convicted us that this was indeed a profound truth for all of us here in Europe.

Unfortunately, when we returned to tape *This is Your Day* in California, we found out that *we* could be in the balance as well!

Because we were staying in America for a further two weeks, Pastor Benny had very kindly allowed us to tape an introductory two programmes in California, as a run-up to the programmes to be taped later that year.

So there we were, in Irvine, California, all sunglassed and suited up on this sunny California morning, about to leave the hotel to film on Pastor Benny Hinn's *This is Your Day* when we were called to pick up a fax from the hotel desk from London.

Goggle-eyed we stared, riveted on the information that had come off the fax machine, our stomach sinking at every new headline.

> *US evangelist pledges 1 million for Christian TV'*
> *'Hinn TV Bonanza coming this year'*
> *'Televangelist who "cured" boxer promises $1 million'*
> *'Holyfield's healer aids Christian TV'*
> *'Expansion in TV religion alarms priest'*

Whoops! We looked at each other, our hearts in our boots— it seemed that the British media had once again decided to set their sights on the Christian Channel and this time had decided to make a meal of Pastor Benny Hinn's unfailing support.

I quote from the *Guardian*:

> *Benny Hinn, the millionaire American evangelist reputed to have healed the former heavyweight champion, Evander Holyfield, has come to the aid of Britain's first Christian satellite television channel with a promise to raise $1 million (£660 000) to expand its output.*
>
> *The involvement of Mr Hinn, a faith healer, who claims illness is of the devil, will provoke criticism that Christian Channel Europe is bringing the worst aspects of American televangelism to this side of the Atlantic.*

Others were more graphic:

Christian Channel Europe, based in the Family Channel Studios at Grove Green, has been pledged one million dollars by flamboyant evangelist Benny Hinn and plans to use the money for big expansion.

In *Broadcast* it stated:

Money pledged by Hinn personally (whoops!) *and from the Eurothon will be funnelled into the Angel Christian Television trust.*

This was *not* the moment to say, 'Oh, by the way, Pastor Benny, just in case you didn't . . . um . . . er . . . know, the British press seems to have heard the announcement at the church service in Orlando . . . and er . . . um . . . it seems that the British media have got wind that that you are intending to assist us, and are believing for a million.

'The only slight problem, Pastor Benny is . . . er . . . hem . . . that we seem to have (cough) is that the British press don't really understand the word 'faith' or 'believe' . . . and some even seem to think that it could even come from your own personal bank account . . . (choke)!!'

Oh, yes, we knew that this was *just* what Pastor Benny wanted to hear. Our hearts were in our boots. So, very honourably, we folded the offending press releases in our now sweaty little paws and crumpled them up into my handbag, waiting for the right moment to divulge this red-hot information to the Reverend Benny Hinn.

There we were, on *This is your day* in California, smiling sweetly at Pastor Benny, with the offending headlines casually stashed away on set, sharing enthusiastically about the Christian Channel, hoping against hope that Pastor Benny's London office weren't about to call frantically in the middle of our programme and tell him about the headlines before we did.

(It amazes me that all of our make-up for *This is Your Day* stayed on, with all the perspiration that must have been pouring off our brows!)

To make matters worse, when we visited Trinity Broadcasting Network (TBN), Terence Hickey, Paul Crouch's right-hand man, had a photostat copy of the article that had appeared in *Broadcast* that week just lying casually on his desk—'*US evangelist pledges 1 m for Christian TV*'.

Now we knew that the news had reached *America*!

'I heard it was five hundred and fifty thousand yesterday,' he laughed, (with us growing a whiter shade of pale) 'but today it's a million!'

He brought the offending article out.

Now all the colour drained from our faces . . . if Paul Crouch knew, then surely Pastor Benny would find out before we got the opportunity to tell him? In fact, Pastor Benny was the one who was helping arrange to meet Paul Crouch.

Pastor Benny might think that *we* had leaked it to the press— an idea so unbearable it wasn't worth thinking about. We were as shocked as we were sure he would be. How on earth did they get hold of this? We had been in America—how had this got out?

However, back over the Atlantic, our creditors were feeling much happier at the thought of a one million injection and the newspaper headlines silenced some of our critics. It was just Rory and I who seemed to have been walking across a diplomatic minefield in California!

Then, to make it worse, we overheard that Pastor Benny never liked to read the press before crusades or ministry.

Now we *really* faced a dilemma. We were just about to show Pastor Benny the articles—what should we do? Give the articles *to* him or keep them *away* from him?

We had hoped on both evenings after the tapings where we were Pastor Benny's dinner guests, to find the right quiet moment to share our dilemma and to show him the offending newspaper clippings. But that quiet moment was not to be and we decided that the wisest route left to us was to share them with Pastor Benny's associate evangelist Ronn Haus, when Ronn came over to set up the London crusade.

On our return to England, Pastor Benny was indeed informed by his British office of the controversy. We met with Ronn Haus at the Metropole Hotel in London later in March, where he told us that Pastor Benny never dreamed Rory and I were involved in the presumptuous statements put out by the press and had not been ruffled by the situation. Instead, Pastor Benny had given us the benefit of the doubt and, gracious as always to God's fledgling television channel, had decided to let the whole controversy run like water under the bridge . . .

Chapter Sixteen

❖ ❖ ❖

Good Morning Europe!

I had stayed sipping cappuccinos in Starbucks in America a little too long, because I have to admit that as the plane veered through the grey murky clouds nearing Heathrow on that Monday morning, I was very tempted to get a calling to Orlando in the winter and California in summer and take the next plane back to America.

Instead, I descended the aeroplane steps and followed Rory reluctantly into Heathrow terminal with the distinctly growing sensation that we were about to re-enter Hellsville and the spiritual frontline in Europe.

Once we were back on British soil, we were bombarded by what seemed to be a hundred varying pieces of information.

We also walked straight into the aftermath of the BBC's controversial documentary on the Christian Channel, *The Miracle Channel* which had been broadcast two weeks earlier, not to mention the articles still circulating in the British press about Benny Hinn's million-dollar faith injection.

The *Sunday Mirror* wanted to interview us for an article to appear in the Easter edition of their colour magazine supplement. (The front cover of the April 7 issue later read '*And in the beginning there was the Good Book. Then cameth the strumming of guitars and those that fainteth in the aisle. Now Christian TV hath arrived and we ask of the multitude: who shall cast the first stone?*')

We had been invited to appear on Selina Scott's talk show on NBC Superchannel.

We were due to be interviewed by Jonathan King of London's Talk Radio.

We had also seemingly been taken to task by the more traditional Christian channel Ark 2, who were seemingly using Ernest Rea's (Head of Religious Broadcasting BBC) comments about us from *Everyman*, as a tool to convince the media that compared to us (the Christian Channel, e.g. American televangelists, overt evangelism, Pentecostalism) they were as harmless as a pet hamster. (We were portrayed more as a rabid alligator!)

But now it was back to settling down to the day-to-day running of the channel and straight away into filming the next series of *Good Morning Europe*.

And therein lies a tale.

In the initial months of the channel's launch, Rory and I had been avoiding appearing *in front* of the camera, but there had been a nagging feeling, which grew stronger each day, that God actually wanted us in front of the camera and not just directing operations from behind the scenes.

But we kept suppressing the Holy Spirit's gentle nudging.

However, by the beginning of December, person after person kept coming to us with a word from the Lord that we should be communicating with our viewers on a programme of our own.

Finally, George Otis (a well-known pioneer of radio in the

Christian world) who was visiting with us, spoke to us quite
emphatically about it, not knowing that we were dragging our
heels.

There was no doubt about it—we were being disobedient to
the next stage in God's plan. We might have to start in a simple
way but start we must. And although it was not the way we
would have chosen naturally to shoot *Good Morning Europe*,
because of our production house background and our aspiration
to excellence for the gospel, we wanted this to be the house that
the Lord built, not just our own good idea.

And that is how *Good Morning Europe* started in our *dining
room!*

On 25 December, sitting on a borrowed sofa (ours was slightly
older), the hired camera rolled and so we started *Good
Morning Europe from Rory Alec and Wendy Alec.*

Now, as our viewers no doubt noticed, Rory took to being in
front of the camera like a duck to water, but without fail, I would
clam up every time! When we played the tape of our first few
Good Morning Europe programmes to my father, he looked at
me suspiciously.

'*What's* the matter with you?' he stared at me in a strange
fashion. 'It looks as if all the life's drained out of you!'

He then proceeded (with a grand twinkle in his eye) to call
me 'Dumbo' (as in dumb brunette!) the entire weekend, not able
to believe how his normally vibrant daughter could appear so
totally devoid of life on *Good Morning Europe*.

Well, they say you get used to cameras, and day by day, I
started to relax . . . sometimes we relax too much!

Then after Christmas, we decided to move to the dining-room
table, which seemed to work quite well, but we still only had
one camera which, adept as Carlos our cameraman is, proved to
be quite inhibiting.

But what fun times we've had . . . from Rory catching me
still chewing gum as the camera rolled . . . the mobile phone

accidentally being left on the table for half the programme . . .
Rory offering me the whole bunch of peach artificial roses in
his hand out of the vase as a romantic gesture and suddenly the
whole of Europe knew they were plastic! . . . and then there was
the time when our cat gaily walked through the open door and
wouldn't stop miaowing . . .

Then there was the morning when we were starting our
introductions and I kept bursting into giggles.

It was getting *so* bad, that Rory was actually starting to get
quite mad at me . . . quite mad continuing into *really* mad as we
reached the sixth take.

'It's the Holy Spirit!' I spluttered.

Well, from Rory's expression, it was quite evident that he
was not at all amused.

'It *is* the Holy Spi . . . ' Another hysterical gale of laughter.

Rory was sitting there, completely furious. (Later he had to
repent.)

For indeed God if we surrender to Him, moves in ways, that
may be foolishness to the natural mind, but the end result is life
for the people. On that particular morning, as on many
mornings afterwards, God wanted to reach out and touch His
people who were suffering from depression, to lift those who
were bowed down.

You see God didn't want *Good Morning Europe* to be a
show—He wanted to meet the needs of our viewers and to inter-
act with them. He wanted us to share with our wonderful and
rapidly growing family from across Europe.

The heart of *Good Morning Europe*, apart from sharing with
you the excitement of all that is going on at the Christian
Channel, is to meet whatever needs our viewers may have as
individuals.

We're there to pray for our viewers, to stand with them, to
welcome them as part of our family and to reach the body of
Christ across Europe, all standing in the gap together.

There are those of our viewers who watch us from council flats, on income support, struggling with the hardship of day-to-day living; there are those of them who have just been told they have only a few months to live by the doctors; there are those struggling with addictions, with habits that they can't seem to get victory over on their own; there are those who are hurting, lonely and rejected . . . and you see, beyond all the letters that we read, and the events, and the Knowing Us . . . Knowing You's—*Good Morning Europe* is for them.

And let us never make the mistake of playing television . . . for you know, the Lord is consumed with the welfare of His people. They are top priority on His list and whenever we do get to go without praying on screen for too long, He gently whispers to us, 'Meet the needs of MY people.'

And then came the response.

On our return from America, we arrived back to over a thousand letters from our extended European family, so excited and enthused with what God was doing.

From Slovakia, Lithuania, Germany, Poland, Switzerland, Austria, Sweden, Norway, Denmark, Italy, Spain, Estonia, Holland, England, Scotland, Ireland, Portugal . . . the letters flooded in.

The testimonies of salvation, of healing, of the Holy Spirit overcoming our viewers, of our viewers' absolute joy at being a part of the Christian Channel family! And the literally thousands of letters keep coming!

Oh, there was one week we taped and Rory and I had just had a disagreement about who on earth knows what . . . we can't remember! . . . Then as the camera rolled and we went through the entire shoot struggling hard to smile at each other, especially me because I can't just suddenly pretend that everything's hunky dory when it's not. Then Rory said how he loves me and I felt like going 'Humph!' to the whole of Europe!

We giggled when we were in Scotland and some new-found

pastor friends were tickled pink when they noticed that there
was Rory blazing with Reinhard Bonnke zeal and fire about
Europe . . . and there was Wendy . . . (they said 'the lights
upstairs had gone out!') looking as if I was thinking about hang-
ing out the washing! (Oops I got caught!)

You see, I have a pact with Carlos. If Rory goes into a *long*
preach—he is supposed to turn the camera onto Rory!

And the time I kicked Rory under the table because he was
just about to divulge a piece of top secret coded CCE information to the whole of Europe. (In fact he did, anyway.) And Rory
said (in front of the whole of Europe), 'Stop kicking me under
the table!'

Oh, we laughed when we were at the 'Catch the Fire' conference in Sunderland, when one of our lady viewers congratulated
me. She thought that I had kicked Rory because I wanted to
talk! (Well, you know, it's hard to get a word in edgeways with
someone who operates under a preaching anointing, but that
wasn't the reason.) She encouraged me to do it more often!

We need to take a tip from Marcus and Joni Lamb who are
far more refined than the Alecs and showed us the last time we
were in America how to get each other's attention very subtly on
set.

Much more subtle than us.

After that conversation at 'Catch the Fire', I had visions of
John Cleese smashing a plate over Prunella Scales' head and
saying, with smoke billowing from his ears, 'Could I have a
word please, *dear*?'

Then there was the occasion when we decided to have a
'Family' Programme as so many of our viewers (mostly the
Christian Channel grandmothers) had written in wanting to see
our children.

So, like a good 'House on the Prairie' Alec Family, we dressed
Christian (19 months) and Samantha (nearly 5 years) suitably
for the grand occasion and proceeded to sit at the dining room
table with the camera rolling.

Apart from Christian continuing to repeat 'Daddy' rapidly all through Rory's introduction, things were going well. Then he kept waving at the cameramen. Still passable. Then he proceeded to issue the strangest set of what could, at a long shot, be passed as laughter, but sounded more like a pig snorting. Christian has never laughed like that before . . . or after . . . but he did that day!

Now, as a mother, I thought that this was the cutest, adorable thing imaginable but Rory had other ideas.

Christian then proceeded to dismantle one of our artificial roses right in front of the whole of Europe.

Scenario—Christian pulls rose head off.

Rory is addressing viewers (slightly agitated).

Christian lets out another unbelievable set of snorting. I try not to giggle.

Rory is still addressing viewers (extremely irritated with us).

Christian pulls stalk of artificial flower in half.

Another long drawn out set of snorting laughter.

I collapse into giggles.

Rory is now furious.

Christian is unceremoniously banned from the set.

Mother is now extremely upset at darling sweet son being expelled.

One gone . . . one to go.

We start again.

Samantha does her bit really nicely.

'Good Morning Europe—God loves you.' In perfect 'House on the Prairie' angelic Christian daughter style.

Then she is instructed to sit quietly while we finish the programme.

Meanwhile, I am now *really* upset that Christian has been banned for snorting and dismantling the flower . . . but I still have to smile because we are on TV. I am not a good pretender and the smile is rather wilted.

Then Rory starts to pray.

There is a strange, undefinable bouncing sound. (Whoops.) Samantha is bouncing from sofa to sofa to our left.

Now, I wonder if Samantha is going to be banned too . . .

Rory continues praying, with furtive glances out of the corner of his eye.

The furtive glances become more ominous.

The camera stops rolling as Rory gives a stern warning to Samantha to desist in the bouncing.

The camera rolls once more and Rory continues to pray for our viewers.

Strange strains of attempted off-key singing filter towards us from the bouncing sofa area intermingled with more bouncing sounds as Rory continues to pray in front of Europe.

Is that smoke that I see billowing out of Rory's ears?

CUUUTTT!

The camera stops rolling and Samantha stops rolling as well! She is now banned up to bed unceremoniously.

Loud wails and sobbing come wafting down the staircase.

Rory looks at me (much happier) and says as the cameras roll 'Wendy, pray!'.

Rory is now much happier but Wendy is much unhappier at both her poor helpless little darlings' expulsions (even though Rory was right).

However—after a cup of coffee, a lot of deep breathing and five minutes break, things were back on track, apart from my extremely feeble and insipid smile throughout the whole next programme.

You see, we're just a normal young family called by God coping with the pressures of ministry, family and running a television channel . . . and the one thing you'll always know about Rory and Wendy is *what you see is what you get*!

And our viewers are real too! Oh, they bless us so by their warmth and enthusiasm. We meet many of them at crusades and conventions. In fact at the Benny Hinn Crusade in London and at the Kenneth Copeland Believers' Convention, we were nearly over-run by our viewers! We were brought cheese from Holland, chocolate from Switzerland, postcards, hand-made gifts . . . one morning even a bouquet of beautiful flowers arrived from Jersey. (Thank you for that wonderful thought—I never was able to find out who they were from.)

And Rory and I are committed to our viewers. The purity of heart and the hunger for God to be found in Britain and Europe at this time is incredible. It is God's time for revival, and revival starts in the hearts of Rory and myself and of each one of our Christian Channel family watching each morning in their living rooms. And together as the bride of Christ, all the flames shall burn fervently across the dryness of twenty-two European nations as a sign and a wonder to this last generation.

What a privilege and an awesome responsibility.

Chapter Seventeen

❖   ❖   ❖

The Dedication

*S*ince the launch of the channel on the first of October, the desire to have a formal dedication of the Christian Channel had grown in our hearts.

It was to be an evening where the Christian Channel was to be dedicated to the Lord in the same way as Solomon dedicated the temple to God after it was built. An evening where God would receive all the glory and the honour for the remarkable miracles He had performed to establish Europe's first daily Christian television channel.

On the evening of the Eurothon in Florida, Pastor Benny had agreed to be our special guest at the dedication and the date was set for 24 April 1996. The dedication would be held in the Westminster Central Hall in the heart of London and our special guests from Europe that night were to be Pastor Colin Dye from London and Pastor Ulf Ekman from Sweden.

As the date neared, the excitement in the Christian Channel

Offices was tangible. All our energies were now focused on the
dedication and the production offices were crammed to bursting
with staff and excited volunteers writing tickets, manning phones,
answering enquiries, sealing envelopes. All with one focus—24
April.

And then came the letter.

We had been through hell so many times before that we
had started to recognise its symptoms when they started to
appear . . .

And, believe me—hell was definitely looming up again in
the form of a letter from the Family Channel who had just been
taken over by the conglomerate Flextech (who also manage the
Playboy Channel) and who were not so kindly predisposed to
Christian television.

The letter said—in paraphrase—that we had thirty days to
vacate the building, hallelujah. (At least we still had five days
after the dedication to do it.)

Now considering that we had received literally thousands of
letters since the launch of *Good Morning Europe* and most of
them were brimming over with excitement about the
Christian Channel, our ACTT 2000 partner base was growing
every day, but not fast enough. We were behind in our Family
Channel bills, by sixty days, and the new owners intended to
take us to task—pay up or move out. (The money pledged from
the Eurothon viewers mostly came in on a monthly basis and
had been used to cover the remainder of the outstanding launch
bills.)

And *now* it got worse . . . they intended to cut our telephone
lines on 4 April . . .

There we were, the phones ringing off the hook with requests
for dedication tickets, inundated with excited callers from across
the British Isles and around Europe, with the momentum
growing every day . . . and we were about to be evicted and cut
off!

That meant that as soon as the dedication was over, we would be moving premises to . . . where? . . . visions of Reinhard Bonnke's tent loomed up . . .

Suddenly, I had a wild vision of our only communication with the outside world being a one-way communication on the screen of the Christian Channel saying 'OUR PHONE LINES HAVE JUST BEEN CUT . . . WILL YOU BECOME AN ACTT MEMBER NOW? ARE THERE ANY MILLIONAIRES WATCHING THE CHRISTIAN CHANNEL? . . . S.O.S.

But, of course, resilient as one surely has to be when pioneering, it was time to get ready for Round Two of the battle.

So later that day, after our faithful accountant, Jonathan MacMahon, had scraped the Christian Channel bank accounts and given the Family Channel a minor cheque (with lots of grace and prayers beaming upward), the phone ultimatum was stayed for a few more days.

But the situation was extremely serious. If we didn't have God's miraculous intervention—24 April would be a *devastation.* not a *dedication*!

But in the midst of all the seeming turmoil, that still small voice echoed, 'Peace, be still.'

Had we not walked far enough with our wonderful *mighty* God to realise that this was just another opportunity for Him to show Himself strong on our behalf . . .

We were once again about to see God's miraculous power change our situation in an instant. And two cold and rainy days later, came our transatlantic miracle, in the form of a telephone call from California.

It was from Terence Hickey of the Trinity Broadcasting Network.

TBN would sponsor an hour's airtime for *Praise the Lord* each Sunday and . . . *this* was our miracle—they would forward the whole six months upfront—now! Enough to pay the overdue Family Channel bill with thousands to spare.

Let me add, that we have never seen American dollars wired

to the Christian Channel bank accounts so swiftly from the United States!

God bless you Paul Crouch, Terence Hickey and the faithful partners at TBN. You know not what you did to help us from the 'colonies' (as Terry calls the USA).

Oh—our God is so faithful.

Nothing could stop the tremendous spirit of joy and victory that afternoon in the Christian Channel. Our God had done it *again* and *again*! Right when it looked as though this was the end— that it was finished—God had turned the water into wine.

And so the phones stayed on, ringing off the hook, and the offices thronged once again with staff and volunteers, writing tickets, manning phones, answering enquiries, sealing envelopes. All with one aim—the dedication.

And then there were no more tickets. Still the phones rang . . . and rang and rang . . . and this was before we had opened the event up to the churches. In fact we had almost a thousand people on waiting lists for overflow. By this time, our faithful production and administrative teams were completely spent. Everyone had been doing two or three people's work from morning to night for the three weeks before the dedication.

Now it was the night before—and we still had to edit the final Partners video for the audio-visual presentation.

So Rory, John Lilley (the editor), Graeme Spencer (our Production Co-ordinator) and myself huddled in the edit suite . . . and morning turned into afternoon which turned into evening which turned into midnight . . . which turned into four-thirty in the morning, whereupon after grabbing the Family Channel's First Aid room pillows, literally bombed out from a week's lack of sleep, I did the cowardly thing and left the boys and crawled into bed.

Rory arrived home at seven-thirty, completely exhausted.

It was Wednesday 24 April—blearily we looked at each other through a groggy haze—it was Dedication day!

So there we were at ten in the morning, past the point of no return, with suitbag in the black Golf, making our way through the London traffic towards the St James Hotel, hopefully for forty winks. (Ha Ha!)

Well, it was obvious there was to be no catnapping, and our destination changed rapidly to the more forbidding site of Westminster Hall. By now, I was in a state of high anxiety (even the peace of God that surpasses all my understanding didn't seem to make a dent in this brand of high anxiety). I had to go on stage in front of a crowd that night. That was enough to make me want to climb back into the edit suite.

There was Rory, gaily whistling his way through the traffic, quite enjoying the thought of sharing on stage, while I would have liked to have been dropped off somewhere near the Outer Hebrides in Scotland. But this what not to be and so we found our parking spot and entered the auditorium.

The screens were up, the sound check was in midflow, the plants had just arrived. There was no turning back.

Pastor Ulf Ekman had just been picked up from the airport. Pastor Colin Dye (our Master of Ceremonies) was meeting at six o'clock with Rory for a briefing as to the evening's agenda . . . and Pastor Benny would arrive . . . (well, we weren't quite sure). Oh Lord Jesus, please don't let him get held up on the wrong side of the Atlantic!

God had showed me that these three men who were the special guests of the Christian Channel that evening were there by divine design. He had also said to me weeks earlier that each had a name that evening.

And each had significance for Europe.

'The Lion' (Pastor Ulf) would roar prophetically across Europe, and foundations and structures even of whole nations would shatter and crumble to pave the way for the new order— the order of God. Even governments and kingdoms would shatter at the roar of God's lion.

'The Dove' (Pastor Colin) would be God's diplomat. He would

be God's peacemaker across denominations, bringing unity of faith to many streams of churchmen in the continent of Europe. He would have a voice in both the kingdom of God *and* in the secular—and so, a great call would go out for unity in the body of Christ . . . The hallmark of great wisdom would rest upon the dove.

'Elijah' (Pastor Benny) would stand out as God's sign to a stiff-necked and unbelieving, intellectual Europe. And when they 'Where is this God you serve, who seems so powerless?' Pastor Benny would come forth as the man of God had long ago, before the prophets of Baal, demonstrating the fire and the miraculous power of Almighty God in this last generation in Europe.

As early evening fell in London, the excitement became tangible as viewers from all across Europe started to queue outside Westminster Hall. They came by bus, by car, by plane, by train . . . but they were there. People came from Germany, from Switzerland, from Spain and Holland. From Iceland, from Sweden, from Austria and France. From Ireland, Scotland and Wales, and all parts of England.

And so this historic evening began—an evening that would seal God's amazing miracle—the birth of Europe's first daily Christian television channel transmitting its signal to a potential twenty-one million living rooms across Europe every day.

The doors opened to over two thousand two hundred highly excited Christian Channel viewers and European ministers who crammed into the building to join together in dedicating Europe's first daily Christian television channel to the Lord Jesus Christ.

Well, there were Rory and I, rushing into the entrance of the St James, and almost bumping straight into Pastor Ulf Ekman (me without a scrap of make-up) and his lovely wife Brigette.

Rory met with Pastor Colin and we arrived back at

Westminster Hall at seven p.m. I can't tell you how incredibly nerve-wracking it was. (Pastor Benny still hadn't arrived.) Everything was poised and ready. Over three hundred ministers were thronging in the aisles, Christian MPs, as well as our honoured ACTT 2000 partners and our Christian Channel viewers.

There I was, hidden in the wings, watching the evening unfold.

Westminster Chapel's walls could not contain the excitement, the anticipation as the Kingsway choir sang the opening song 'Jesus is alive!' And as the lights dimmed and the first audio-visual rolled, no one was disappointed. Even from backstage, our viewers' claps of absolute delight as clips of the programmes were shown could not be contained!

Next entered Jennifer Hughes, CCE's vivacious presenter for CMTV (Christian Music Television), still bubbling over with excitement from her trip to the Dove Awards in Nashville. Jennifer introduced Gifted, one of British Christian music's shining young rap artists who performed his latest song. Pastor Colin Dye followed to a delighted roar from the crowd. His eyes were gleaming with exhilaration.

'They said it couldn't be done,' he surveyed the crowd. 'The response that you have shown tonight as we have seen some of the favourites from the CCE broadcast (we had played the audience our promotional reel) demonstrates the fact . . . ' (Colin took a breath) ' . . . that Britain is ripe for the pure, radical, anointed, Spirit-filled, biblical message of Christian truth!'

The crowd erupted into applause.

Pastor Colin went on to introduce clips of the Christian Channel's *Thought for the Day* programmes featuring many well-known ministers from the British Isles, including our much-loved Reverend Wynne Lewis.

'Wendy,' Rory came and grabbed me. 'It's nearly time to go on—Pastor Benny's arrived.'

I did not show great enthusiasm.

Now, actually, if the real truth be told, I had another reason for becoming scarce and herein lies a confession. Not a *full* confession, just a partial one, enough to confess that I had received a communication from a certain pastor's office in Orlando stating that that same pastor was most displeased with Wendy Alec. The matter revolved around an over-entrepreneurial fax to that same office (unfortunately written by WA; signed by WA; all roads leading back to WA).

No prizes for guessing right. It was a certain Pastor Hinn.

(At dinner later that week at PB's favourite Arab restaurant, I discovered that it had all been a *complete* misunderstanding— all was forgiven!)

But I didn't have that inside information—and so a certain Wendy Alec would have preferred to walk out on stage *minus* courteous introductions to Pastor Benny and his entourage. In fact, Wendy Alec would have quite enjoyed watching from the wings all night. (Coward.) This might have been Pastor Benny's day, but it wasn't mine!

And so, a chastened Wendy Alec, a bubbling Rory and a completely at ease Pastor Benny and Ronn Haus all came out to face the dedication audience.

Well, to make it worse, just as Rory and I and Pastor Benny's party were seated on stage, the sound started to do incredibly strange things . . . then there was a hitch in the audio-visual . . . Oh, how Rory and I cringed inside at every strange and incomprehensible (and deafening) sound from the PA . . .

But for all the behind-the-scenes anxieties, this was a night of tremendous significance on God's agenda for Europe, and as Rory and I walked forward to greet all our viewers, we were once again overwhelmed by the tremendous responsibility and the tremendous privilege that God has granted us in entrusting us with His television channel.

You see, at the end of the day, only one thing counts and that is that God's will is being done. There have been many times of heartache and discouragement, as well as those of great triumph and headiness, but on every occasion that Rory and I have been tempted to become blasé or complacent, we have quickly realised that this is God's channel, not ours and that the blessing and anointing rests on it being His to accomplish His purposes on the earth and not our own.

It is so easy in the hectic pace of pressurised, high-profile ministry to touch the glory meant for God alone. But He is supremely jealous over His servants, be they Pastor Benny Hinn, Pastor Ulf Ekman, Pastor Colin Dye or Rory and Wendy Alec. And as Rory and I met the 'generals' of this generation, the over-riding hallmark of God on their lives across the earth has been that, without exception, they give God *all* of the praise, the honour and the glory.

As we went on stage, there they were—all our wonderful viewers—face to face and once again the whole reason for the existence of the Christian Channel came into focus—the *people*.

To meet the needs of God's people.

To comfort those who mourn.

To bind up the broken-hearted.

To reach out to the back-slider.

To preach the gospel to every creature.

To bring the hope of the gospel into the living rooms across Europe.

For God's heart yearns for His people. And God's heart yearns for the back-slider. God's heart *yearns* for the pre-eminently wicked bound by the shackles of sin.

Rory asked for the house lights to be put up so that finally all the faces of the Christian Channel viewers could be seen—and what a sight they were! Our valuable and precious Christian Channel family *in the flesh*.

Then he did the unthinkable and Pastor Colin Dye was the *willing* victim. Using Colin as a visual aid, Rory proceeded to explain the importance of television as a powerful tool to preach the gospel to the masses of Europe.

Colin with unfailing good humour, in balletic pose, teetered precariously on the chair until Rory let him off the hook!

And now it was time for Pastor Ulf Ekman to stir up the viewers as only this *lion* of Europe could.

'How will the light come into the darkness?' he demanded.

'Because Europe has been the dark continent,' he hesitated. 'Not Africa, but Europe.'

'In the second chapter of Joel, we read about the army of the Lord moving forward, jumping over the walls, jumping through the windows, taking people captive.'

Pastor Ulf knitted his brows.

'Where are they? How will they do that? How can we jump over a wall? How can we jump in through a window like a thief and steal them for the gospel?

'We can do it through television!'

The crowd erupted as Pastor Ulf let loose his special brand of Hallelujah fire.

'Hallelujah!'

'A baby is being born tonight' (he took a more serious tone). 'There is no ordinary night . . . '

'There is a calling. There is an anointing, but there is a mandate,' Pastor Ulf hesitated. 'And when the mandate really comes forth for something; the devil can never stop it—I believe that is what is happening tonight.' He stared intensely at the crowd.

'This is not just television—it is not just a channel—it is truly a channel for the Holy Spirit, to teach and to train, to touch millions of peoples and their lives in every nation . . . ' His eyes flashed with fire . . . 'In this *wonderful* and *great* continent of Europe!'

The lights dimmed and slowly Pastor Benny came on stage to an uproarious welcome.

Oh—how our viewers love him.

'Tonight we're here for a heavenly, divine purpose,' he said softly. 'This is a divine appointment.'

Pastor Benny bowed his head.

'Je–sus.'

The audience came to a hush as the presence of God descended throughout the auditorium.

'We thank you for this miracle that you have performed . . . ' (He hesitated and continued quietly in that tender, lilting tone which he uses when he speaks to the Father.) 'As great as the miracle of the feeding of the five thousand—putting this incredible ministry together in Europe.'

And the anointing started to fall. So gently. So tenderly. A sweet, sweet presence of the Holy Spirit. As God the Father's hallmark on His infant channel—the Christian Channel Europe. 'To you belongs the praise—to you belongs the majesty—to you belongs the glory.'

He closed his eyes.

'Father God, you birthed this ministry—supernaturally you did it—I pray tonight that the anointing of your Spirit will not only come but rest mightily upon your work here in Europe . . . ' (There was a silence as Pastor Benny quietly stood in God's presence.) ' . . . in Jesus' name.' Then Pastor Benny turned to Rory and me.

'And the word I am going to give both of you is from the Scriptures, for the Bible says in the book of first Corinthians that God has not chosen the great things of this world but the foolish things and the weak things and the things that are not to bring to nought the things that are.' He gestured to us.

'And tonight, you are looking at a couple—probably the most unlikely couple to do what they are doing—but God has a purpose in all this . . . '

For you see, dear reader, in the same way that God used David the shepherd boy to slay Goliath, and Joseph to save the nation, God still delights today in using the weak and foolish things of this world to bring to naught the things that are.

And so God chose to use a young man and woman from another

nation, unknown in Europe with no money, no powerful organisation behind them, no credibility or influence, with just one phone line, one fax and the Word of the Living God to launch Europe's first daily Christian Channel that would broadcast it's signal every day to over sixty-five million people and across twenty-four European nations.

It is the story of David the shepherd boy, who stood before Goliath with no armour, no gleaming sword or medals of honour . . . it is the story of Moses, stripped of all his Egyptian prowess and it is the story of Rory and Wendy Alec, unlikely candidates in the natural, but chosen by God for His divine purpose.

It is the story of heartache and discouragement, of seeming defeat turned time after time into overwhelming triumphs and victories.

Above all, it is the story of the Living God, the God who *delights* in the impossible, the God who healed the leper, who fed the five thousand, who parted the Red Sea, who raised Lazarus from the dead.

For more than our story, it is His story. He is faithful to His children beyond measure . . . and all the praise . . . and all the honour . . . and all the glory goes to the God of our Lord Jesus Christ—the *glorious* Father.

For ever and ever..
Amen . . .

And the story has only just begun.

> *'Not by might, nor by power, but by My Spirit,' says the LORD of hosts.*
>
> (Zec. 4:6)

Prayer of Dedication

(This is the prayer used at the dedication service on
24 April 1996 at Westminster Hall.)

*We dedicate the Christian Channel in the Name of
God the Father, God the Son and God the Holy Ghost
For the work of the Kingdom of God
For the glory and the honour of Jesus Christ
For the honour of His Name
To proclaim the gospel
To Europe and the world*

*Father God—We vow before you, Jesus
We vow before you, Holy Spirit
We vow before the holy angels
We will give Jesus the glory
We will give Jesus the honour
We will give Jesus the praise*

*God of Abraham, Isaac and Jacob
Anoint the Christian Channel with the Power of the Spirit
in Jesus' Name
Destroy Satan's plans
Destroy his works in the lives of millions
Establish your truth in the lives of millions
Establish YOUR truth in the lives of millions*

*To you be the praise—to you be the glory—
to you be the honour—for ever and ever
So be it—Amen*

A Reckless Example of Living by Faith

The Church of England Newspaper
—Friday 3 May, 1996

Christian Channel Europe was dedicated at a lively charismatic meeting at Central Hall, Westminster, on 24 April.

I was not there on behalf of this newspaper, but as the personal guest of the founder Rory Alec. In an almost reckless example of faith, they are running a fully licensed television station without even a television camera (they hire one). Yet they have managed to pay £100,000 worth of bills on time each month.

It was a supreme irony that just the day before I was in the Church Commissioners board room for an Investment Committee meeting discussing the millions managed for our pensions board.

It is clear that most of the channel's support comes from the evangelical Free Churches. In my pride of place (middle of the second row at the front), I was surrounded by black Pentecostal pastors who greeted me warmly.

In answer to 'and which fellowship do you lead, brother?' I told them that I belonged to an obscure religious sect called the Church of England. As there were over 300 pastors present that night, I still do not know why I was accorded such pride of place.

One curiosity about the independent charismatic churches is that they treat their pastors like pop stars. As they appeared in succession on the screen, different groups of 'fans' would cheer. The loudest cheers were for Benny Hinn, who was top of the bill that night and seems to have the status of Take That.

There was a curious gospel rap artist called Gifted, dressed in boiler suit and overcoat. I hate rap music, but must admit he was good.

Eventually, and late, it was time for top of the bill—so please welcome Benny Hinn, cue lights and music. I had not seen or heard Benny Hinn before that meeting, but had heard extreme views for and against him. I was just looking forward to seeing for myself, just ten feet away, whether he had horns or a halo.

He was given a rapturous welcome, which he clearly expected. It was almost a disappointment that he is just an ordinary preacher. There was nothing he said or did that might give me the slightest cause for concern. It was a bit overtheatrical, but he is American. He led the meeting in a simple prayer of dedication for the channel. I was happy to take part.

As an act of worship, it was not exactly Choral Evensong. But it was a wonderful evening—relaxed, good humoured, lively and totally committed to the gospel.

I attended with what I hope was an open but sceptical mind. I was particularly on the look-out for pressurised demands for money, exaggerated claims of healing, or any wonky doctrines bundled in with the gospel. I heard none—not the faintest hint of them.

People were invited to give money to the channel, but with no more wild claims than would be made in any parish church appeal.

The channel's policy is to preach the gospel, uncompromisingly and honestly. And they practise what they preach.

As a worldly accountant, I think that this channel is hopelessly underfunded and under-resourced. It seems destined to fail; indeed it should never have started.

However, as Christians, there comes a time when we must use the gift of discernment to look beyond the wisdom of this world. This channel is already being transmitted daily to 25 per cent of all homes in the UK. This is not a pious future hope—it is simple current reality. I was unmoved by all the 'psyching up' at the meeting, but I was impressed by the simple honesty and obvious conviction of Rory and Wendy, and those around them.

I honestly believe that this channel is the handiwork of God. Just occasionally Christians—even Anglicans—must step outside our worldly wisdom and conventions and recognise that God is doing a new work in a new way.

This is such a work.

Robert Leach

And the Letters Flooded In . . .

'Glory to God!—We send you our abundance of love from Vienna! Christian Television has been desperately needed in Europe—Praise the Lord. He has done above and beyond anything I could ask or think. I believe you will be a vehicle for a mighty outpouring of restoration and healing!'

Susan
Austria

'I love to watch the Christian Channel. This is my only food in this country!! I am your supporter.'

Michael
Czech Republic

'You'll not know how miraculously your programme has saved me from destruction and Hell. I am a Christian and I almost deserted my family and faith. On 9 February I was in my front room watching your programme and all of a sudden the Holy Ghost quickened my inner spirit to be alive unto God.'

H. A.
London

'Praise God! Through my listening to the Christian channel—I've taken steps to confess my sins and I know God has saved me.'

Doris
London

'I used to watch the Sci-Fi channel, smoking pot and taking other drugs—then CCE would come on and I'd watch it for a while. Soon I was watching it for longer. This was the REAL Twilight Zone, the real Star Trek and Christ was the real (Multi) Million Dollar Man!!'

Paul
Notts.

'For exactly two years I have been a very lapsed Christian. I let my sins carry me away from God. One night like many of your viewers I was channel hopping and came across muscular men breaking bricks on stage (The Power Team). Now I am getting up at four in the morning to be spiritually fed. I can't thank you enough for your faith, trust and vision.'

Mark
Lancashire

'Recently I awoke early from another night's restless sleep and chopping across the channels I discovered the Christian Channel Europe. This morning I prayed the Sinner's Prayer with Wendy and believe I am a new creation.'

Andrew
Wallington

'I am a very constant viewer of this Christian television channel. I have now received the Lord as my Saviour. I have stopped drinking and smoking 'cos the heart must be clean and made holy for the Lord Jesus Christ so that he can live in me.'

Leopold
Germany

'I've just watched your channel for the first time and thank the Lord for such a wonderful channel—it has changed my life around. I prayed the sinner's prayer with you both and it was like a great weight had been lifted from my shoulders. Before today, I suffered from depression that I could see no end of, but now it is gone and I am filled with joy!'

R. J. West Midlands

'Wendy and Rory, I believe I speak by the Spirit of the Lord when I say to you that the advent of the Christian Channel Europe is spiritually the single most significant event to have taken place in Europe since Martin Luther's day and the Reformation. Just think what that means! The second and final spiritual reformation of Europe has begun. Glory to God!'

Julian
Bath

'*Good Morning Europe* touched my heart. It brought back deep feelings within myself. Feelings that I had forgotten.

'I have been in England several years now and have backslidden badly. I don't belong to any church although I did try. I didn't make it. Seeing your programme caused me to weep in repentance.'

George
Rochdale

'It is privilege that I can address you with greetings and thankfulness for your courage and commitment to serve the Church in Europe. We heard long anticipated news and today we are first in Lithuania who advertise your programmes in Christian periodicals, translate your programmes and offer to send them to different churches and denominations.

'We are SET AFLAME with your idea and work, for we believe with all our hearts it is God's work!

Pastor Donatas and Nijole I
Lithuania

'About six weeks ago, I started watching the Christian Channel and since then I have found a new way of life—the way of God.'
Derek
Scotland

'What a GREAT BLESSING it is for us to receive your satellite programme daily. Since then we tell everyone we come into contact with or write letters so that others can have Christmas in their hearts every day because of the Word of God coming over the airwaves through the Christian Channel.'
Dorothea & Gerard
Berlin

'God bless you young Rory and Wendy Alec! You cannot imagine—just guess—how much you and your/our(!) Christian Channel means to me and a lot of people throughout Europe!! Imagine my great joy, when flipping the channels early in the morning some time last December, I FOUND YOU! '
Erna
Sweden

'I receive your wonderful programme through the Astra satellite. I prayed one month before you start the broadcasting daily. Your work is a good work. God bless you.'
Josef
Nuremberg

'Your channel is excellent in every way and a true blessing to the people of Europe—it will save many and become one of the most powerful instruments that our Lord and Saviour, the Lord Jesus Christ, will use in these latter days.'
Alasdair
Scotland

'I want to let you know that someone is watching in Portugal from the very first day. I thank God it happened in my life during a very dry period. I can say it was a miracle. Christian Channel happened just in the right time. I couldn't believe God is good and he loves me. I say like Pastor Benny Hinn 'that was MY day!'

Grace
Portugal

'I'm so glad and thankful for the Christian Channel Europe which I receive via the Astra satellite! I and many other believers prayed for full gospel TV here in Germany! After the sign off of the Christian Channel I was so full of joy and deep peace and I had to cry too! Please do continue with these programmes especially the ones with Brother Copeland, Brother Hinn and the fine music.'

Peter
Germany

'This is exactly what we've been praying for—a supernatural outreach into Britain to change the spiritual climate.'

Pastor P. F.
Cheltenham

'What a blessing it is to see you flowing with God's purposes for Europe. Now is the beginning of this special season. So here YOU ARE—right on time in God's plan, bringing good teaching, lifting our faith and helping the children. It is as Ulf Ekman said 'Europe shall be saved!'

Andrew & Carole
Gibraltar

'I was in despair for we didn't have these programmes in France. Now you have brought to us the Christian Channel in Europe!

You cannot imagine how happy we are! God bless you and your team!'

Minh
France

'I have to write and tell you that I got my best gift on New Year's night. I was just looking at what was on the TV. Maybe there was something interesting. I got a very big surprise. I found your Christian Channel and it was the best gift to me for 1996! I am so excited and will tell about you EVERYWHERE!'

Sanna & Bjorn
Faroe Islands
(Islands in the Norwegian Sea)

'WOW! You know preachers need to be fed spiritually and this is a FULL supply from God! I thank the Lord for using people like you to do His wonderful job. God bless you in your ministry. If you ever come to Lisbon, please let me know.'

Jorge
Portugal

'We are Christian workers in Morocco who have a parabolic antennae, as most Moroccan citizens do now. We were happy to stumble on your Christian television network!'

Karen & Dan
Morocco

'Words cannot tell the joy I had when I discovered the Christian Channel. Here in Hungary, there are lots of people longing for revival for the outpouring of God's spirit. I record the programmes and then gather my friends who don't speak English and have no satellite dish and watch it together and I have to tell you that we feel the presence of God watching the programmes just like those do who are on the conferences, and feel very very blessed!'

Dora
Hungary

'We are glad to be a part of what God is doing in the lives of His children through the Christian television Europe. We in Italy, have been feeding from the spiritual food made available to us every morning. It is so great to wake up to the presence of the Lord.'

Mr and Mrs I.
Verona, Italy

'I very much appreciate the work you are doing leading the Christian Channel Europe! It is amazing what God can do through a Christian satellite channel!'

Joachim
Sweden

'I thank the Lord for the way he has used you both to launch Christian television in Europe. I videotape the programmes and circulate them amongst my English-speaking friends and hope to start a library so that I can make the tapes available to church groups. Switzerland has no Christian programmes and therefore this channel will be a great blessing to them.'

Pat
Switzerland

'My family and I are very grateful for your broadcasting all over Europe and hope to take part in all this exciting growth. You bring us great joy and fill our house with praise every day— Praise God for your ministry.'

'I am writing to tell you that during one of your transmissions I was born again. A week or so ago, Rory stopped reading a letter and stated that he was aware of somebody watching who had tears in his eyes. He went on to explain that this was the person of the Holy Spirit and he prayed for him to receive it. THAT PERSON WAS ME!'

Steve
South Glamorgan

'For the last three years I backslid and turned away from God and since I've been watching CCE I have repented and recommitted my life to Jesus. '

Alan
Cambs

'My wife and I experienced a near awakening of the truth of the Gospel and for myself it came at a time when I was beginning to despair. Through your Christian Channel we are both enjoying a new lease of life in the Lord. My fears have been replaced by a feeling of hope and contentment.'

Dennis
West Midlands

'I came to the Christian Channel by accident by just flicking through the channels to see what films were on and came across this new channel. I didn't know what it was about at first until I was hooked. I believe now that it was time for me to be saved.'

Andy
Lincolnshire

'I was brought up as a Roman Catholic, but only ever paid lip service to my religion, probably because I was forced to go to church. Recently events have occurred which have really made me struggle with any belief I have had in God. This morning I prayed with you. I have never done this before and did not ever expect to. I cannot begin to describe to you the feeling I gained from this, but I suddenly feel happy . . . '

Steve
Somerset

'I thank God for the Christian Channel. We had been backslidden for three years. We are now both attending our fellowship again. Thank you for giving me back my relationship with the Lord Jesus Christ. Whenever I've tried before to return to Jesus, I have always failed—but now I'm back on the right path and I am all out for God 100% . . . '

Jacquie
Edinburgh

'I was just screening through my satellite channel around 7.45 precisely this morning when I caught a glimpse of your programme *Good Morning Europe*. I was touched by your inspiring word of how our Lord and Saviour Jesus Christ will take control over Europe and the world at large. I recognised for the first time in my life that I am a sinner and need repentance.'

Al
Germany

'Watching the Christian Channel has literally changed my life. No longer do I watch depressing, boring and compromising secular TV. This is what heaven will be like, God's word all around!'

Christine
West Yorkshire

'I laughed, I cried and prayed with the two of you and now I know in my heart and soul that all of these things were for me to come back. My son left the room when I watched the Christian Channel, now he watches and has brought books and is overcome by the power of God and Jesus has certainly touched him!

Stephen
Dorset

'I had lost the joy I had when I first knew the Lord and was born again. Just before Christmas, my married daughter said, "Mum, there's a God channel, shall I tape some of it for you?" Since then the Lord has lifted me up and given me fresh promises, filling my heart with joy and answering my prayers.'

Carol
Cheshire

'The second of May became my day. I was set free from a very strong fear I have had since childhood. I was not only set free from fear, but I was also born again. It all happened when Wendy prayed for people with fear. My whole body was trembling. My husband said, "You have been set free, Susanne." I said not only the fear, I am also born again!'

Susanne
Denmark

'Please consider us a Christian Channel church. We are flipped out and flying high on your programmes! Everyone of our church members gets to see the broadcasts both via a lending library of morning programming that we have set up and also our Thursday night video ministry night. Thank you for all your help and wonderful service to the Body of Christ in Europe.'

Pastor S. M.
Cheltenham

'Thank you very much for the new TV channel, we are so thankful for the work you have done and are doing to bring the gospel out to the population of Europe. I have worked to get the Christian Channel known here in Denmark and especially in Hjorring. Through articles in newspapers and contact to the local cable operator, it is now succeeded so the Christian Channel is on the local net, so today 10,000 households are able to see CCE if they hire a decoder!'

Pastor S. J.
Denmark

'I cannot begin to express what a difference CCE has made to my life and that of my friends. We seem to have developed a mini-ministry in lending out videos of the broadcasts. After so long surviving on so little we are overwhelmed by the abundance of excellent preaching.'

Karen
Yorkshire

'Like many viewers I pass many of the tapes onto my friends in my local church who do not have satellite and the feedback is of great interest in what the CCE is doing in spreading God's word and the blessings that it is bringing.'

Tony
East Sussex

'We confirm our interest to retransmit and distribute your programmes in Poland. If you find time to come to Poland we would be very happy to receive you.'

P. J.
Warsaw

'We also operate a cable network with about 12,000 subscribers. A lot of these subscribers have asked us to distribute the Christian Channel Europe in our network.'

T. S.
Jakobstadsnejdens

'Every morning I record all the programmes separately and continually circulate them with the people who do not have the privilege to view this telecast. Healing, deliverance, understanding and growth is found. These tapes are doing a great work for the Lord. We have also helped friends to switch cable TV on in order to view.'

New Malden

'We decided to make our commitment from our local church group here in Basildon as part of our outreach for souls. We all

share the videos of each day on CC. I wrote to the local cable
network in Basildon and they put you on in November so much
of Basildon can receive you now.'

Alan & Shirley
Essex

'I have recorded every day your programmes on video tape and
with your leaflets passed them out into the local churches so
people can know what God is doing in England and Europe.'

David & Pauline
Cheshire

'I have been showing some of the video recordings of *This is
Your Day* to the people at a fast food restaurant. They want to
see more!'

Patrick & Debbie
E. Sussex

'The Lord has given me a vision to post the promotional leaflets
for your channel into EVERY home in my town who has
satellite. As requested, I have asked for another 400 leaflets but
will in all reality need three and a half thousand!'

Andrew
Scotland

'We have one dear brother in our fellowship who faithfully video
records your broadcasts every day and the videos are passed
throughout the whole church on a rota basis so it can be up to six
weeks before the whole process is complete!'

Sam & Pam
Wiltshire

'I have distributed 500 or so leaflets and factfiles of the
Christian Channel to half of Worksop. Today I received a supply
of factfiles only. I really do enjoy going around my town

searching out the satellite dishes and popping these "seeds" into people's lives. I would be prepared to continue in this work possibly in the neighbouring towns and cities . . . '

Tony
Notts.

'The videos are lent to a number of friends, neighbours and relatives who are thrilled with what they see. So word is spreading fast and you should be increasing your audience rapidly in the near future if my experience is anything to go on!'

Tim
Leicester

I've received some *88 hours* of Christian Channel broadcasting for my own use: and when I've finished with the tapes, I pass them on to others.

I can't afford to buy the satellite equipment because I'm unemployed and on income support.

These videos have been recorded for me by a friend at the church.

Charles
Sussex

'Warmest greetings in the lovely name of Jesus from Eastern Europe! We were very happy to find out that you're broadcasting even into Eastern Europe via satellite. We watch *This is Your Day* and the Lord blessed us and encouraged us for all day long. Praise the Lord! We love you. See you in heaven.'

Lubo
Slovakia

Update

An exciting update—our cable distribution in the United Kingdom has increased from 300,000 to over ONE million cable households!

The testimonies of salvation, healings and renewed lives continue to flood in from as far away as Finland and Estonia.

Lithuania shouts *Christian Channel come!* . . . as does Poland and Slovenia . . . and the Czech Republic and Bosnia . . . as does Germany and Switzerland, France and Italy . . . Denmark shouts *come* as does Norway and Sweden . . .

Whole churches all across Europe are watching the Christian Channel Europe. Many have started libraries (some with up to three hundred tapes of the Christian Channel). Housegroups are watching from Paris to Berlin; from Madrid to Oslo; across Hungary and Slovakia; in Lithuania and Romania and throughout the Eastern Bloc; from John o'Groats to Land's End in the United Kingdom. Christian Channel tapes are being played in womens' groups and youth groups; in prisons; in Sunday schools and Christian schools. A US Army base in Germany is tuned into the Christian Channel Europe; soldiers from the peace-keeping force in Bosnia Herzegovina are watching. Rough, tough men watch on oil rigs and fishing trawlers in the North sea. *This is Your Day* tapes are being played in a fast food shop in Sussex. Sceptical spouses, friends and neighbours are being saved as they tape the channel for Christian relatives. Believers all across Europe are inviting non-Christians totally set against Church and religion into their living rooms to watch Christian television. Drug addicts are being born again. Sci-Fi fanatics are being born again as are teachers, bus drivers, single parents, teenagers, agnostics and atheists. Morocco is watching, Estonia is watching, Belarus is watching, Bulgaria is watching. Whole churches in Kenya are watching (on videotape!)—all hungry for the Word of God—hungry for revival.

For God has raised up The Christian Channel Europe as a new tool of evangelism in Europe—a tool that will break up the fallow ground of unbelief and intellectualism—a tool that will crush in pieces the strongholds of darkness and beam down the searing light of the gospel through the heavenlies that until now were ruled by the principalities of the power of the air. A new era has dawned and the season of the first fruits of revival is about to be ushered in—for surely righteousness has started to rain down from the skies, watering the dry and barren continent of Europe.

We, at The Christian Channel Europe are committed to take the message of salvation—the message of the gospel of the Lord Jesus Christ to a lost and dying Europe.

The fields are ripe unto harvest.

Who will go?

. . . We will go.

ACTT

What is The Angel Christian Television Trust?
The Angel Christian Television Trust (ACTT) has been the
vehicle to launch The Christian Channel. The Channel is a
conduit, the delivery mechanism which is the culmination of all
the fundraising, gifts, donations, physical and spiritual energy
put into the Trust.

How can I support the Trust?
By becoming a member of ACTT—a group of evangelicals personally committed to the development of the Angel Christian
Television Trust, from all walks of life and from each part of
Europe. To become a member of this group, we ask for a few
areas of personal commitment, but also ensure we are able to
pass to you many on-going personal benefits.

We believe the many people God leads to become members
of ACTT will not only be valuable friends of the Trust but will
also play an important part in helping the Trust to spread the
Word of God in its television outreach.

Purposes
*   Primarily the advancement of the Christian Faith through the
    televisual media.

*   The advancement of education through the televisual media.

*   The relief of poverty, distress and sickness through the
    televisual media.

Goals
To establish and/or support a Christian Television Channel having regard to the following criteria:-

1. A Pan European Channel to be made available to the general public throughout Europe.

2. Broadcasting on each day of the week.

3. Transmission by all means available e.g. Satellite and Cable.

4. The Channel to be non-denominational.

5. The Channel to adhere to a doctrinal basis being the Scriptural and Historic Apostolic Faith common to the mainstream Christian Churches.

6. The Channel to broadcast a wide range and diversity of programmes.

7. The Christian programmes broadcast on the Channel shall be for the "advancement of the Christian Religion" and any supplementary programmes to fall within two other charitable categories viz.

   a) for the advancement of education.
   b) for the relief of poverty, distress and sickness.

8. The funding of the Channel to be derived from all appropriate sources e.g. by appeals to Churches and associated organisations, Foundations, Trusts and to the public at large and by advertising, sponsorship.

9. The Channel to aim at having a distinctive European character and to encourage the production of its programmes in Europe.   Initially it is anticipated that American programming will need to be used as very little European Christian programming exists.

10. The Channel to proclaim the gospel of the Lord Jesus Christ using all acceptable forms of presentation including those of a contemporary nature. The Channel to have a special concern to show the relevance of God's Word to everyday life and the effects of the Holy Spirit upon people's lives.

Objectives

1. To develop the Trust as a permanent fundraising organisation.

2. To engage upon all the appropriate methods of raising funds compatible with the Christian nature of the Trust.

3. To carry out surveys and research as may be considered desirable to further the work of the Trust.

4. To publicise and raise the awareness of Christians to all the opportunities and potential of the television media for the effective communication of the Christian faith.

Strategies

1. To recruit all necessary voluntary assistance for the day to day running of the Trust.

2. To draw up a rolling plan of action for fundraising schemes after carrying out any necessary pilot surveys.

3. To establish a panel of Reference whereby the Trust will consult with such a body on matters to be specified in its terms of reference. The panel will include places for persons to be nominated by various Christian Churches or their representative organisations.

If you are interested in becoming a member of ACTT, please complete one of the forms below and return it to The Angel Christian Television Trust, PO Box No 397, Maidstone, Kent, ME14 5YE, United Kingdom.

I/We will commit to monthly giving by standing order of £ .... per month, commencing .... for a minimum of 12 months.

I/We enclose a cheque for the first month (£ ....) and understand that a standing order form will be sent by return to enable me/us to support the Trust on a regular basis.

Signed   .... Name: ....

Address: ....

.... Postcode: ....

Tel. no: ....

If you do not feel you can become a member of ACTT at the moment, but would like to help, please fill in the following:

I/We would like to make a donation of:

☐ £50   ☐ £25   ☐ £12   ☐ £5   ☐ Other

Signed   .... Name: ....

Address: ....

.... Postcode: ....

Tel. no: ....